GameBreaker

GameBreaker

Guide to World-Class Selling

Developing the Personal Brand
Defining the Extraordinary Salesman

Ronald G. Brock

Galt/Mirrin Publishing

First Edition, Second printing
Published 2022

Galt/Mirrin Publishing
Printed and distributed under the auspices of Galt/Mirrin Publishing, LLC

Edited by Louise Harnby
Cover and Interior Design by Ghislain Viau

ISBN Paperback: 978-0-578-18504-0
ISBN eBook: 978-0-692-79109-7

Library of Congress Control Number: 2016917574

*"Your value depends on what you make of yourself.
Make the most of yourself, for that is all there is of you."*

—Ben Feldman

Table of Contents

PART FIVE

Game Communication

PART SIX

Making Time Work For You

PART SEVEN

Putting It all Together

Preface

While writing GameBreaker I was frequently asked if the topic was, "How to Sell." The answer was, "Yes, but more correctly about how an untrained individual can transform into a salesman of notable superiority."

Presumably you are considering selling as a career option, or are already engaged in developing your sales competence. Either raises a reasonable question: how do you develop expertise attached to extraordinary selling success? GameBreaker's gist extends beyond *How to Succeed at Selling*, to *How to Become Worthy of Success*.

Possibly a few characteristics associated with a salesman's image were inherited. If your crib was blessed by a visit from the sales fairy, presumably your life has followed a predetermined path resulting from such good fortune, and now holds your destiny. But, recognizing that geniuses are born to every profession, if you weren't born a Larry Fitzgerald, a Renoir, or an Einstein ... GameBreaker was written with you in mind.

Among organizations of any type, people are selling something to someone, most of the time. The selling pros who earn their livelihoods by carrying the company banner are high-profile. But what about those who need other's cooperation to make a pet project happen? They sell their ideas.

Selling is a primal art. Like acquiring skills needed to play a sport, selling skills are nearly always acquired. There are people born with a few natural capabilities, but most begin a sales career as relatively ordinary. For these people, success isn't a result of an accident of nature, but a natural consequence of mastering the subject.

New experiences are among our culture's most highly valued commodities; nowhere more apparent than as applied to professional selling. For the more ordinary aspirant to selling, life occasionally delivers an epiphany, an *aha* moment with a sudden realization you can do something that once seemed remote. That was selling to me.

When it became apparent I could do this, and found there was great pleasure in the activity, selling had me. It was a game. And I loved the game's challenge. The excitement of searching for a sale, and the satisfaction of having found it, is unique to selling, but the process is not always understood in the same way.

Playwright Arthur Miller's Pulitzer Prize-winning Broadway play, *Death of a Salesman,* characterized a salesman as a chronically unsuccessful individual named Willy Loman. At age 63, after 37 years with his company, Willy was fired.

Willy had held tightly to the conviction, key to great selling success was likeability, even as he consistently failed at the activity.

GameBreaker turns to Willy's polar opposite—the archetypal über-successful salesmen—and the path these exceptional individuals have followed in becoming consummate examples of professional selling's *best in the business:* people like Ben Feldman.

An uncommon story of a common man, Ben Feldman became among the selling profession's acknowledged most dominant salesmen ever. He didn't begin that way.

As applies to any skilled profession, acquiring Ben's selling proficiency is no accident; rather, a result of a masterfully executed plan. A quest of sorts, complete with a hero, and obstacles to be overcome.

Experience has shown that a majority of aspiring salespeople begin an intended career path without first consulting a roadmap. For most, individual nature also presumes they feel they are *not like anyone else*, therefore must find their own way. Correct assumptions—both counts; selling skill is acquired. For some, skills seem to be more easily developed, while others struggle to find their mark.

For either, the ultimate objective is acquisition of a competence similar to the skill achieved by an individual who has chosen to extend his athletic capabilities beyond an amateur's, to those capable of competing at the highest level—the dominant type who becomes a professional athlete.

New thoughts posed in literature on selling technique, most particularly by, or about, someone who has experienced notable success at the activity, piques our enthusiasm. I am intrigued by people who have been successful at what they do, and are willing to share their secrets to success.

Many books have been written with the author's opinion of, "how to do it." And an abundance of *how-to* books on selling technique have promised great reward if *this simple pathway to success is followed.* Over a 50 year span I have made personal reference to many, including such classics as: Og Mandino's *The Greatest Salesman in the World;* J. Douglas Edward's *Questions are the Answer;* several of Zig Ziglar's books, including *See You at the Top*; and Dale Carnegie's, *How to Win Friends, & Influence People*.

I found that many contemporary sales-process definitions included some interesting concepts, but didn't address developing the personal brand attributed to individuals who succeed in making the profession a career. More importantly, failed to address how to develop the behaviors capable of transforming selling from an occupation into a profession—and transforming a person of seemingly ordinary potential into extraordinary competence.

Selling, like professional athletics, is a solitary profession, spent in the spotlight; an individual's actions make things happen, or they don't.

The ticket to succeeding is available to just about anyone committed to making selling their profession. But achieving "A"-list status in selling's hierarchy, people who inspired this book, results from acquiring a collection of skills in dealing with an array of challenging conditions.

Individuals who achieve remarkable selling success range in type from very private, almost secretive, people who understand the value of silence and unobtrusiveness, to boisterous, overbearing, too-talkative characters who like to be in the middle of everything.

Both groups have in common they are determined, and are universally optimists. Individuals of high character, they are risk-takers, seek challenges, are talented, and make the most of what they have available to them. And they see selling as quite a simple thing: it is play.

It also became apparent to me that almost anyone with the desire, and dedication to do so, can become an effective salesman. In time, a great salesman may be born.

GameBreaker is about becoming that person.

Acknowledgments

I am a salesman. For my entire business career, that's how I made my living.

The career path I chose had its share of dragons and moat monsters, all of which were necessary to delivering an experience which evolved into as much avocation as vocation. I loved being a salesman in the way a professional athlete loves his sport.

My career began with direct sales, transitioned into sales management, marketing management, and ultimately business startups. I am privileged to have been associated with an array of sometimes remarkable people—as mentors and associates. Most provided examples of what to do; some, what not to do.

It was clear, if not from the start, then soon after, individuals who had achieved sales profession dominance possessed certain distinguishing qualities. These remarkable individuals, people who define the term, *GameBreaker*, established dominance in their geographic area.

One such role model in preeminence was Ben Feldman. Discussed in Part One, Ben transformed himself from a less than remarkable small-town egg salesman into the greatest salesman to ever represent

New York Life; for that matter, one of the greatest salesmen to ever sell anything for any company.

I know Ben only by his reputation, but was privileged to witness in action several individuals who dominated their areas of activity with Ben Feldman-like competence as commercial real estate brokers. Most notable among this eminent group are: Tyler Anderson, Jeff Hawk, and Sean Deasy in the Western United States; Malcom McComb and Jamie May in the Southeast; Scott Melnick, Al Cissel, and Bill Roohan in the Mid-Atlantic; and Matthew Lawton in the Midwest.

Those "A"-list examples of extraordinary competence were supplemented by studies on human behavior completed by sometimes groundbreaking researchers who unknowingly pointed to some useful insights, capable of enhancing the selling process.

There are too many to name all who played significant roles—mentors who extended beyond simply serving as managers, to positively affecting ways of seeing a few things differently.

But it would not have been possible to have worked through the occasional challenging times without the unwavering support of Carolyn, the wife who endured with considerable patience a career-long series of mostly interesting, sometimes disturbing, challenges, and resulting outcomes.

And in the process a few things were learned, some that may be of use to you.

PART ONE
THE GAME

CHAPTER ONE

Selling as a Profession

The term, *Selling,* is applied generically to occupations involving one individual facilitating a business transaction between parties, or to promoting an idea to others.

And, like most forms of employment, selling is subdivided into relative degrees of required sophistication, each participant becoming progressively more expert in their particular niche.

As a result, the definition of *salesman* is applied loosely to a variety of activities: retail clerks, route salesmen, automobile sales, high-level product sales (airplanes, main frame computers, locomotives …), to the sale of products facilitated by cold calling—an array of construction-related products, business machines, life insurance, real estate, industrial products …

This group's more passive components wait for a customer prospect to approach, another has a route book listing accounts to call on at some established frequency. Still others are counter salespeople who work from a catalog of products, and have responsibility to process an order when a customer calls. In selling's echelon these categories occupy the ladder's lower rungs.

3

While participating individuals within these groups are capable of differentiation through demonstrated competence in relation to peers, *GameBreaker* is dedicated to selling's pinnacle—individuals who have distinguished themselves in competitive cold-call selling—and how to acquire the skills consistent with those exceptional individuals.

The Professional's Game

Becoming an upper-echelon salesman requires acquiring a few new skills. Not necessarily Parade All-American, Super Prep, render-Dick Vitale-speechless skills, but basic talent, and a pure commitment to succeed will be of considerable value toward achieving the objective.

In selling it's not the commodity being sold, or the work itself, that's important. What is important is the process, how it looks, how it behaves, how it accomplishes what is intended, and its adaptability to the moment's enterprise. This departure from the snake-oil days of selling ("just make the sale") to a more customer-oriented view is relatively new.

Salesmanship has only within the past 50 years evolved from a cliché-ridden *("plan, do, review." "questions are the answer ... ")* activity into a well-defined profession.

Today's highly orchestrated selling tests the salesman against constantly changing circumstances. A structure of this sort is called a game. And, like any game, selling has players, a language, history, rules, controversies and a certain rhythm. As a profession, also potentially well-compensated, compensation increasing in proportion with the circumstances' perceived disagreeableness and relative risk, and the salesman's competence in dealing with the circumstances.

In this game (referred to from here forward as *The Game*), two players participate: the salesman, and the circumstances. The circumstances are composed of a sale prospect, the prospect's related needs, and the at-the-moment business/personal environment.

The Game board is any venue in which The Game is played: direct calls, tradeshows, web-enabled, telephone contacts …

The Game's rules and terrain are relatively straightforward, but strict. Selling income is generally performance based, exactly a game in every sense the word is used.

Effective response to the circumstances gets paid. To win against the circumstances you become stronger, or smarter. In The Game the latter prevails.

The Game is one of trial and error. As experience progresses the trial and error becomes more sophisticated, but never ends. Some will be better at it than others; some will achieve dominance.

With all you will find someone who, exercising the salesman's legendary persistence, continued on when discouragement heaped on discouragement was the moment's order.

And with all who make it their mission to become very good at selling, the ultimate reward is in playing The Game well. Not the statistics. Not the trophies. Just the enjoyment of having achieved the ability to do what you do well.

A reasonable understanding of motivational psychology's application to the selling process is achieved by The Game's dominant participants, the *GameBreakers*. Representing the best of the sales breed, GameBreakers are characters of many dimensions, definitely no two alike. You know them—individuals everyone turns to when a tough job needs to be done right—and right away.

The Salesman Profiled

Selling success results from developing a special skill of being consistently able to urge a decision from a sale prospect.

A salesman's characteristics are, like those required of a quarterback, a mixture of courage, toughness, instincts, preparation, resourcefulness and a few other less tangible variables. And, as applies to quarterbacks, every salesman is different, a special case; the sample size, always one.

The salesman's image is alternately romanticized, and vilified, neither viewpoint entirely correct. Spontaneity, intense emotion, attractive appearance, outgoing personality, instant persuasion at the drop of a hat ... all contribute to the positive view of a *born salesman's* image.

This destined-to-be-a-salesman type shares an image with politicians—substance not required—heavy emphasis on form. Form—outgoing personality, attractive appearance—is to selling what cosmetics are to the face; substance is what diet and exercise are to the body.

The born-salesman cliché does apply to a minimal percentage of the population, but has no connection to performance. With a natural sense of how to influence other people's feelings toward them, this type *can* become an excellent salesman.

But if the born-to-be salesman relies on form's halo effect as a substitute for substance a selling career will be hard-put to leave the launch pad.

Born-sales-type personalities have a natural attraction to sales, and populate lower echelon selling positions; as politicians they may become president of the United States. But the born-sales-type may have difficulty with what composes the substance of an individual capable of dominating selling in the manner a sports star dominates his field.

For individuals not *born* to be salesmen, but who have chosen selling as a profession, substance—an ability to make things happen— is the ticket to performance. A salesman's substance is developed through acquiring key behaviors supporting personal effectiveness, combining those skills with professional knowledge.

Among the best of the sales breed, GameBreakers are recognizable for readily apparent *confidence* (knowing whatever life tosses at them, they will be fine), *composure* (ability to think clearly when things get rowdy), and *competence* (handling difficult circumstances with unruffled dignity).

Developing the personal product required of a competent salesman can be simplified to a few essential characteristics:

The ability to confidently pick up the telephone and call someone, or walk into an office unannounced and ask for the decision-maker;

Superior listening skills;

Ability to place others at ease;

A Midwestern farmer's work ethic; and

An imperative for action.

If self-evaluation leaves you short, there is no need for concern. These traits are seldom natural; nearly always acquired.

Playing The Game

The Game is one of subtle skill.

As with an expert poker player, decision-quality separates Game experts from amateurs. The salesman's advantage is control of the transaction's direction, elevating outcomes from a crapshoot, to something considerably more in his favor.

A new player has a preconceived agenda, his own slant on things. But for most, the agenda is based on a range of untested assumptions about The Game, most having little to do with how The Game is actually played.

Selling, like most games attaching serious outcomes, is only won consistently by the pros who have made it their mission to become accomplished at what they do.

What makes The Game so interesting is the circumstances are not a shy opponent; you will be challenged. The slightest error can result in the ball being spiked in your end zone. You can prepare for that.

Of-the-moment circumstances can be unpleasant, even borderline unacceptable. But, whatever they are, they are never as they *should be*, or as it would be preferable for them to be; they are only what they are at that moment.

To deal with any circumstance, judgments regarding preferences are set aside. With the circumstances accepted, you can now work with them as if you had personally chosen them.

In *The Book of Survival, Everyman's Guide to Staying Alive ...* author Anthony Greenbank observed: "To live through an impossible situation, you don't need the reflexes of a Gran Prix driver, the muscles of a Hercules, or the mind of an Einstein. You simply need to know what to do."

The Game requires several roles played. A driving-force behind promoting a product or service is assumed. But there are the roles of planner, administrator, facilitator ... some part of the day extending beyond conducting business to supporting what you expect to bring to the event tomorrow when The Game is resumed.

Gut-level techniques and strategies that work most consistently are seldom natural, more usually acquired. Developed capabilities provide instinctive response when winner-takes-all is the outcome: powers of observation, assertiveness, ability to read other's nonverbal language, and a particular array of habits and behaviors to be made instantly available when The Game is on.

It will probably be necessary initially to act in ways that you may have thought you were too shy or polite to act. But those are self-placed limitations. With that recognition, you act to develop a *self* that will do the work.

The contrast between you as you are now, and *you* as a seriously capable Game participant, is the difference between a YMCA pick-up basketball game participant, and the select few who earn their living in the NBA.

The occasional no-nonsense type is capable at the outset of playing The Game exactly as it was intended. But for most, until a satisfactory Game strategy can be developed, borrow one. Follow an expert. Many of The Game's best players have fashioned themselves after a mentor who has achieved notable Game success.

You may not lift the exact way someone does something, but you can adapt a similar pattern. The Game style you develop may be a lot like, but will not be exactly like, others. The herd holds remarkable similarities. But no exact clones.

No two people are alike transitions into *no two salesmen are alike* or participate in The Game in exactly the same way. To say that all salesmen are alike is as absurd as insisting that all music sounds alike. Competent individuals apply the same basic rules, the difference is in how each goes about it.

The fact is, selling is more art than science. It requires order, but also feeds on a certain randomness, and constantly challenges. A prime sale-process component is failure, the kind you learn from.

The Human Quality of Perseverance

The successful salesman fails more often than the unsuccessful salesman. For a different reason.

The unsuccessful salesman sees failure as defeat; the successful salesman knows succeeding requires failed attempts. And remarkable success attaches a greater number of failed attempts, a concept not unique to sales.

Among all activities dependent on developed skills, mistakes made are essential to achievement of impressive outcomes. The typical professional baseball player hits to reach base less than one in four times at bat. Ted Williams, one of baseball history's greatest players, achieved a career batting average of .337. He failed to hit for first base nearly seven of ten times at bat.

Succeeding results from commitment to accepting nothing less than accomplishing what you set out to do. If there is a single outstanding argument for all-out personal self-improvement pursuit it's represented among individuals who have achieved remarkable success. This high-functioning group typically performs their work for the pure pleasure of the activity—recognition is secondary.

Successful salesmen begin a transaction with succeeding as a mindset. Failures don't change their attitude. They become more determined—push, strain, compete, double the effort, redouble the effort, triple the effort …—whatever is required. They are universally individuals who persevere after others have abandoned what they determined to be a losing cause.

Discussed by philosophers since the beginnings of written Western thought, perseverance—a synonym for persistence—is a highly regarded human quality. Its genesis is not certain—only that as a quality for succeeding when times are difficult, persistence's value weighs heavily on outcomes.

Persistence can be mistaken for aggressiveness, but is significantly distinguishable: aggressiveness is the pursuit of a position at all costs; persistence is assertive, an unwillingness to give up when emotions are screaming, "Quit!"

Both are statements of a not-to-be-denied attitude, but aggressiveness may be overbearing; persistence is not loud, boastful, self-promoting, seeking to promote a pet project, or view. It just won't be denied.

The subject of perseverance has been examined from every conceivable angle—*winning attitude, burning desire, will to succeed* ... every metaphor leads to, you have to have *it* to prevail.

The Game's day-to-day activity is rife with setbacks. How those circumstances are dealt with arises in part from an internally based series of hang-ups waiting to throw you off track. At its base—one of anyone's most definitive emotions—fear.

Perseverance is most needed when circumstances challenge. Having only your thoughts and feelings to guide you, you are most likely to commit errors.

After you recover from having your feet kicked out from underneath you, a new set of feelings which you may not have been capable of experiencing before, now inspires getting off the floor and trying again.

Mistakes are temporary momentum killers, also superior teachers. A mistake made, and the mistake's cause understood, supports acquiring the personal characteristics needed to deal with similar circumstances.

Dealing with the Circumstances When The Game is On

The Game requires steering by the stars within sometimes disturbingly in-motion conditions. How you deal with circumstances will define whether difficulties encountered are obstacles, or simply inconveniences.

A powerfully defining personality element determining an individual's capacity to deal with challenging conditions lies in viewpoint: the glass is half-empty, or half-full; the world is friendly, or hostile; you are in control of your destiny, or the winds of fate have you at their mercy.

Life's natural order imposes give-and-take. Most people handle a good day reasonably agreeably; the challenging days may raise the question, "Who are those people? And why are they so agitated?"

The Game requires occasional encounters with difficult-to-deal-with individuals. When accommodating one of these types, or the resident know-it-all genius, there is no rational support for taking their behaviors personally. Rather, you develop responses capable of steering circumstances more favorably toward your position.

When the bullets start to fly, a disagreeable individual is encountered, or an in-the-bag sale blows up, you find how you deal with your emotions—as the windshield, or the fly. Two poles-apart options will define the outcome:

You, as the gladiator rise to the occasion. Circumstances are assessed, thoughts gathered, a determination made. Sword drawn, you *are* Attila's descendant.

The knee-jerk alternative, dissolving into central casting's image of a spineless wimp.

Intensity is a requirement. Approached with a take-no-prisoners attitude, growth in competence required to consistently deal with the circumstances' near infinite array of subtleties will be steady. And, with growth, incrementally more rewarding.

A little fight-or-flight tendency is a part of anyone's personal make-up. But things must be placed into perspective before acting. The circumstances having asserted themselves, knee-jerk isn't an option. It's show time!

CHAPTER TWO

The Game's Players

Defining Personal Effectiveness

Notable success at any game ultimately lies in art—everything that can't be translated into numbers and facts. You will come to know it as *personal effectiveness.*

There is no clearly prototypical definition of what a salesman *must be.* But there are plenty of definitions of what *can't be,* under any circumstance.

Every salesman is a complex web of habits, behaviors and attitudes, defining an apparent *personality.* But beyond personality something else—human will, *want to*—determines whether outcomes will be mediocre, or there will be a determined emergence from the pack as a formidable participant.

Much of anyone's self-image is reflected in their work—what they do, and how well they do it. What effective Game participants lack in flash, they compensate with:

When the circumstances deal problems, actions define outcomes. If the grade-school bully regularly backed you down, those days are over.

The knowledge that being a prisoner of past history isn't necessarily preordained. Old habits and behaviors decided without The Game in mind can be modified.

An understanding that customer decisions are less rational, more emotional, than may have been assumed.

An intensity of effort required to achieve personal objectives.

The essential importance of a lights-out "selling prototype," a personal *brand* defining the bundle of capabilities acquired for the event.

A maturity to avoid being sucked in by the moment's emotions when things don't go as expected.

Beyond base qualities, an array of character-dependent qualities are common to high achievers:

Self-discipline	Restraint under duress
Integrity	Enthusiasm
Powerful work ethic	Balance in activities
Absolute self-reliance	Optimistic outlook
An open communication style	Patience

Ability to persevere in the face of obstacles

Ability to readily adapt to circumstances

Society tends to categorize. An endless variety of answers to the statement—*there are two types of people ...* is often about winners and losers. No need to deal with the in-betweens, individuals who see *good enough* as their personal standard. Attention is placed here on two ends of the spectrum: individuals exhibiting extreme substance, and those who are notably inept.

At the competence scale's pinnacle, GameBreakers dominate in the manner a junkyard Doberman commands his domain. Individuals holding the supremely confident demeanor of The Game's best—GameBreakers—expect to be accountable for outcomes.

The scale's lower end is populated by Pretenders who, barely making it through the tryout stage, never perform well enough to make the team.

A considerably different worldview defines the two:

The Pretender—attempting to do something they are ill-equipped to do, Pretenders exude an easy-to-get-tired-of undertow in their behavior, supporting such terms as *ruthless, weasely, deceitful* … often applied in opinions describing a salesman in the term's least complementary understanding.

Like dogs incapable of resisting a fire hydrant, Pretenders always seem to be chasing a big deal. They call every assumed prospect after reading about the prospect's plans in the newspaper, which, due to some unfortunate circumstance, the contact never materializes.

A Pretender is more likely to be incapable of accepting a particular circumstance not to his liking as it is. It follows that such an individual will not be able to accept anyone as they are, or any other trying condition as it is. If the option instead is to judge, criticize, label, reject, or attempt to force a change in the circumstances rather than dealing with whatever conditions call for, this individual has little chance of achieving even a standard of mediocrity.

Pretenders are easily recognized, illustrating a cobbled-together garage-band approach to whatever they do, their day ordered by work done only for what they can get.

Customer prospects too frequently ask for things the Pretender doesn't know how to give, or for services they are unwilling to provide. The Pretender's limited capabilities have a similar affect on the Pretender's relative achievements as rocky soil and poor climate have on a farmer's fortunes.

The Pretender's likely attraction to The Game is to pursue the money, an easy way to get by, or possibly some sort of perceived, but considerably premature, glory. A Willy Loman protégé, the Pretender is the individual playwright Arthur Miller described as "Getting by on a shoeshine and a smile."

Typically, Pretenders: don't concern themselves with connecting with their prospects; do not possess the will to become very good at what they do; nor feel a willingness to be held accountable for their failures.

The GameBreaker—a really get-after-it sort. The GameBreaker is an individual with a purpose of notably ambitious proportions. Not someone you expect to find playing Las Vegas' slots.

These high-powered individuals often don't live up to the popular image of a salesman. Rather, they are as likely to exude a cool, inbuilt superiority, individuals who quietly go about their work in a manner completely opposite to the outgoing *everybody-loves-me* type making up the born-salesman cliché.

Personal characteristics often attributed to a *sales personality*— personality the size of a Montana ZIP code—outgoing, flamboyant, full of fun—are not universal to GameBreakers.

Consistent with the stereotypical image of a salesman a GameBreaker can be the sort who gives the appearance of taking daily shots of testosterone—volatile and emotional, projecting a powerful presence.

But GameBreakers can just as well be a straightforward type, full of idiosyncrasies, possessed of a no-nonsense style, serious, ultra-studious, and completely disciplined. People are drawn to them for their superiority of technical knowledge, and thoroughness of approach to their activities. Oozing competence and quiet confidence, the sales task is performed by this GameBreaker-version with Ivy League thoroughness.

Both individuals subscribe to the philosophy, *whatever it takes.* And each near universally has a system, is sensitive to others, is considerate without being fussy, displays a well-developed power to endure, and inspires others' trust and confidence. Most individuals who achieve notable success—those representatives of society's *winners*—share the GameBreaker's attitudes and behaviors.

Both are endowed with an audacity and self-confidence exhibited by great performers among all professions. One might be the top-down, hard-nosed, kick-ass, and take-names-later type; the other, more reasoned, less emotional. One becomes one type of salesman, the other, the other type.

It's not that one is weak on enthusiasm, or the other has no analytical capabilities. It's just that their strengths are on opposite sides of the spectrum—one, primarily emotions, the other, primarily strategy. Each represents a radically different side of selling's human equation.

Both combine distinctive genius with a unique set of flaws. And both have *what it takes* in the best sense of the phrase. You have seen them—elemental beings who act as pure force:

Possessing extraordinary capability for gaining control of a situation;

Knowing they are the ultimate force behind positive outcomes;

Maintaining a near constant imperative for action;

Recognizing that circumstances are never the same;

Knowing there is a younger, just as cold-blooded, player always moving to challenge the reigning gunslinger;

Knowing when the habit behind a behavior is positive, thinking is not required to perform an action appropriate to the moment's demands;

A bad day doesn't trigger a horizon-filling stampede, succumbing to negative thoughts; just, regrouping for a new day.

Knowing that most things don't work the way they are supposed to, GameBreakers eliminate such negative behaviors as fearfulness, a tendency to easily anger, excessive anxiety, lack of self-control, or self-indulgence.

There is no easy road to becoming a GameBreaker. It's challenging. There are quiet sales types, and bombastic sales types. Some are analytical, some impulsive, some tough as nails, but all display a common grit—an intense drive for personal growth, and to succeed at what they do.

If you didn't find yourself described in either category, that's expected. But your personal product has to move away from the Pretender's weaknesses, toward the GameBreaker's strengths.

CHAPTER THREE

Developing the Personal Product You Plan to Become

Game Effectiveness

A mong The Game's most important rules is acceptance of every contingency the circumstances have to offer, then developing the competence to deal with those contingencies.

Extreme personal effectiveness doesn't develop overnight. But if Game effectiveness does not come as easily as you expected, no cause to fret. Muddy beginnings are usual.

Acquiring behaviors the circumstances impose is highly competitive. Obsession with a desire to do a first-class job is a good start. You strive to become the sales version of a sports star. A few personal challenges will not necessarily be a problem, but when:

Thought processes are disorganized, activities will be random;

Personal style illustrates a brash, patently unsupportable demeanor, the outcome won't work any more effectively for you than it has for anyone else;

Attention is diverted from providing exceptional service, to income expected or personal notoriety to be achieved, results will be compromised;

Desire for a sales position is to have more freedom to pursue other activities, intensity required to compete will be impaired;

Product knowledge is limited, so will be effectiveness;

Certain habitual and behavioral changes are required to compete, make the changes.

Game success is achieved not because successful individuals are smarter; rather, they simply combine a rock-ribbed self-reliance with the savvy needed to achieve what they want. Malcolm Gladwell in *Outliers* put it as*:*

> "You only have to be smart enough. Once beyond that threshold it's all application and hard work."

Achieving GameBreaker status is rarely due solely to raw talent. Success comes from the considerable substance associated with superior individuals.

GameBreakers are simply better prepared, and willing to extend themselves to meet whatever the circumstances require.

How Substance Trumps Form—Every Time

A Game career significantly depends on others' willingness to accept a salesman's premise.

A *first impression* is arrived at quickly. One aspect, *form*, is appearance; the other, *substance*, is communicated by what is said, how it's said, what is done, and how it's done.

Some individuals near effortlessly leave a positive impression—never at a loss for words, always the right toast for the occasion. A gift usually attached to a magnetic personality.

Other *gifts* are endowed by birth: attractive appearance—in a man, tall dark and handsome; in a woman, suntanned, statuesque; or talents relating to athletic skill, musical ability, artistic ability, exceptional intelligence.

People born with more than an average share of one or two of these may, as a result, develop an affinity for a particular activity.

But few people have a perfect body, can solve a complex mathematical equation without a pencil and paper, or are naturally charismatic.

A potential drawback to having been born with the advantage of one or more of these socially valuable attributes is, during that individual's formative years, the benefits of popularity may assume a narcotic effect. What came naturally on the playground can have dulled the sense of need to achieve through competition. It came too easily.

Form—attractive appearance, or presence of natural talent—unquestionably opens doors. But if impressive form conflicts with actual capabilities, the individual may go through life receiving opportunities consequent with form, followed by failure when substance fails to materialize. Better to have been born average.

Substance is what the world remembers and reveres—character. Substance derives from: ability to speak well; the backbone to take an unpopular position against a roomful of people when you are confident you have taken the right position; an insatiable desire to learn; a commitment to excellence; delivering on what was promised; subordinating personal interests to what's right ...

Early in my career, it was my good fortune to observe one of these *born-with-it-all* individuals in a corporate setting. Bob was Hollywood's perfect image of a corporate executive. He was in fact engaged to appear on occasion as a corporate executive model in print advertising.

Perfectly straight pearly white teeth, prematurely gray, neatly-cut hair, athletic build, smile a cross between a cannibal and a piano, and a magnetic personality. Dress was impeccable; never less than perfectly groomed.

At a piano bar Bob was instantly engaged in conversation. He was the best singer (baritone, of course) and entertainer in the bar. He was up-to-date on the latest jokes, and a master at telling them. He was a man's man. Success, his for the taking. Or so it seemed

That cultured exterior masked limited character. He was a salesman by vocation, but showed little interest in his business, or knowledge of products; he relied on glib style to get by.

A good talker, he was not much of a listener, but well-spoken. Communication skills were applied more to manipulate than to discover a prospect's needs. He was Willy Loman, with movie-star panache.

Appearance worked for Bob, as he managed to achieve mid-level sales-management stature. His position—as he saw it—was to hire salespeople to work for him (training beyond the bare minimum was not regarded as important). When pressed for an assessment of his sales group's activities he would tell senior management whatever they wanted to hear. This worked to a point.

The streak broke when the president of a company division observed that Bob would make an ideal candidate to fill a national sales-manager position, and recruited him based on a positive impression.

But it wasn't long before old habits showed in performance. His form, which exhibited apparent attributes, lacked substance. Bob had achieved *Peter Principle* status: he had arrived at his self-imposed level of incompetence.

New responsibilities required sales-activity planning, administering results, and reporting of activity. Worse, he was directly accountable for sales results.

For someone possessed of such stunning incompetence, the result was devastating. He lasted just long enough to develop a new reputation—as profoundly lacking in substance.

It was an unlucky day for Bob when he was elevated from middle management to a senior management position. A now recognized lack of substance resulted in a career spiraling steadily downward. The same condition was realized in every new job—termination from a position which never should have been filled by Bob to begin with.

Within the same corporation I received another significant object lesson while attending a sales meeting at which our company's Assistant National Sales Manager spoke. As a recent college graduate, still filled with a starched sense of unsupported self-importance, I was readily critical of appearance that insulted my perception of proper form. I looked up to people who appeared the part, and only mildly tolerated those who didn't.

When the Assistant National Sales Manager was introduced, he presented the appearance of a discount-store shoe clerk. I, of course, was instantly unimpressed. Then he spoke.

The living image of someone to be ignored—possibly disdained—turned into an exceptionally well-spoken individual. He could have set his talk aside, read the Los Angeles telephone book to us, and kept his audience's rapt attention through the alphabet.

My respect for the power of speaking well, coupled with knowledge, was born. This individual had taken substance to such a level, and overcome form so definitively, as to be tantamount to a small boy winning the NBA slam dunk contest. I left that event impressed.

But old perceptions are not easily converted. I did not become a born-again substance junkie that day. But with time, and a few more examples of such extremes (although these still remain the best), understanding came.

Today I am a believer. Not a perfect example, but a believer. And that's all you can expect of yourself. What is clear between these two extremes—all form, or all substance—is most people fall somewhere between the two.

An individual with good form—attractive appearance, always on time, knows the right things to say at the right moment, when to pull out the chair, open the door for someone, offer to buy a round of drinks—impresses.

But, once inside the door, substance—integrity, professional knowledge, creativity, analytical skills, communication skills, dependability, power to persevere over difficulty, positive attitude, and performance—always carries the day.

If you are among the 99% of the population that wasn't born with Sean Connery's style, or any of his 007 female acquaintances' otherwise, opportunity to improve on form is still there—in behavior and appearance.

Distracting mannerisms (annoying accent, poor speech syntax, nervous tick) can be overcome; good grooming, appropriate dress, ability to listen … are available to everyone.

Good manners don't require an attractive face. Good grooming will win out over mediocre appearance. Becoming well-informed on a subject, and capable of stating a point succinctly, is learned. The shoe clerk puts on his Superman costume, and brings out the guns.

So what happened to our two examples? Last I heard the Assistant National Sales Manager was Vice President of Sales and Marketing for another national company. He was undoubtedly recruited based on a well-earned reputation of uncommon capability. And what of Mr. Form? I never saw Bob again, but a mutual acquaintance did.

While on a recruiting trip to New York City our mutual acquaintance was waiting for a taxi when an empty cab pulled up, and Bob got out. He was looking for a job.

You likely can think of examples of both extremes personally encountered. But the population majority is composed of average people, performing in an average manner, in average occupations. But achieving simply average status is too high a price to pay.

Since most people's appearance is neither repulsive, nor possessed of movie-star quality, the opportunity to improve on form is not particularly challenging. Substance comes as a result of attention given to the effort; selling success, a short step away.

One such example—Ben Feldman.

A Real-Life GameBreaker—Ben Feldman

It's not just about what GameBreakers do differently; it's how they think. Great salesmen typically have monumental egos, and love to perform. Above all they are very assertive.

If you were looking for a parable pointing the way to success in selling you would need to look no further than one of selling history's most notable real-life GameBreakers, Ben Feldman.

One of the acknowledged most productive salesmen who ever dominated The Game, Ben Feldman represented New York Life Insurance Company as a life-insurance salesman. At least that was the company's expression of the product they offered. Ben had a different take: "I do not sell life insurance, I sell money. I sell dollars for pennies apiece. My dollars cost three cents per dollar, per year."

The son of immigrants who had settled in Eastern Ohio, where they dealt in junk and poultry, Ben dropped out of high school at his father's insistence, and was selling eggs at ten dollars a week when he met Fritzie Zaremberg. Fritzie's response to Ben's marriage proposal—"How are you going to support me?"—apparently provided lifelong inspiration.

Ben's insurance-selling career began shortly before World War II. As happens to fledgling insurance agents, he quickly tapped out his friends and relatives, requiring new prospects. So his focus turned to owners of small industrial corporations located in the Eastern Ohio/ Western Pennsylvania area. This fertile ground became the standard for Ben's *most probable* customers.

Those prospects, headed by ambitious young men building families, homes, and businesses, were Ben's fair game. Ben dedicated his career to solving what he saw as their universally pressing need— protecting those assets with life insurance.

As they grew, he grew. Other salesmen may have focused on the same clientele, but found themselves trumped by a competence peculiar to Ben.

All insurance salesmen face one near-universal perception—well founded, critics argue—life insurance is not a particularly good investment. But Ben didn't buy into the concept.

In his view an array of ambitious young businessmen were not just well suited for insurance, he truly felt he was helping them meet a need. That conviction, and an understated confidence in his belief that he had a mission to fulfill, served as a driving force behind everything he did.

He wasn't secretive about his techniques. He told other insurance agents—including potential competitors—they could sell more, and he convinced insurance companies to raise the bar on what they would underwrite. When he was beginning his rise as a salesman of note, New York Life Insurance Company would not insure a life for more than $500,000, a limit Ben eventually pushed to $20,000,000.

Without traveling more than 60 miles from his home in East Liverpool, Ohio, a town of 13,000, Ben sold more life insurance in a day than most agents of the time sold in a year, more in a year than most agents sold in a career. In the 1970s it was reported he personally wrote more business than 1,500 of the nation's 1,800 life-insurance companies.

"If I don't buy it, I can't sell it." So he kept buying until he had $6,000,000 in life insurance himself. He framed life insurance as being about life. People didn't die, they "walked out," as in, "When you walk out, the money walks in."

Work ethic was not a problem. He worked 12 hour days, six or seven days a week. He would drop in on four or five prospects a day. Strangers, but he knew all about them. He had scoped out their plants, ordered a company financial profile, and chatted with other clients about the prospect.

He would sit up late, crafting *power phrases,* a series of word pictures that he used so effectively, and rehearse them with a tape recorder. Ben was known for setting apparently unreachable sales targets, then breaking them down into achievable steps—a certain number of calls per week, or so many signed policy applications per month.

He achieved one goal after another: New York Life's Top Agent (1955), the first agent to write a million dollars in new business a month (1956), the first to write a million dollars in new business a week (1969), the first to write two million a week (1975) ... all Michael Jordan-like achievements.

Beyond a clear vision of what he had to say, Ben, notably eccentric, possessed the rare quality of having no problem whatsoever in interrupting someone's day if, in Ben's opinion, it was to their unmistakable advantage. He was equally aware that it was to his clearest disadvantage not to do so. What he may have lacked in other areas he made up through audacity, and dogged determination.

As his approach to a most-probable customer was conceived, Ben's strategy was clear: "I rarely use the telephone because he may not want to see me. I have a better chance of seeing the man I want to see if I go. Besides, switchboard girls and secretaries have become very good. They've learned to take you apart. Who? Why? What for? What company? You don't always get by. I seldom call on the phone. I'd rather go ..."

"On calls, I just walk right in ... and my first barrier is usually the switchboard operator, or the receptionist. On the phone, a switchboard operator can stop me dead. But face to face, the odds are I'll get by. And when I go, I may leave something with her. You know what it is? It's a pair of little golden slippers. She doesn't know what they are until I've left and she's opened the box. Then I usually get a thank you note. From that time on, I get in ..."

"I'm very frank, very open. I just say I want to meet her boss, whatever his name might be, (and you'd better know his name). The receptionist ordinarily announces me, but it's a cold call, and the odds are he doesn't want to see me. I get thrown out of more places ..."

"There are many ways of saying, 'No.' He probably won't see me the first time. That isn't so bad. Why? *Because I'm coming back,* and when I come back I'm no longer a stranger! I've been here before!"

"If I call once or twice more, and the answer is still 'No,' she'll probably begin to feel sorry for me. Now she's on my team. She'll do her best to open the door for me. Particularly if she feels I'd be helping her boss. You've got to have disturbing things to say to the receptionist that will make her boss want to see you, just as you have disturbing things to say to the boss himself."

There has never been a more definitive illustration of pure perseverance. And Ben's notable *I-can-do-this*, style was supported by a powerful belief in his personal responsibilities to his craft, and his customers:

"Work hard. Think big. Listen well."

"Your value depends on what you made of yourself. Make the most of yourself, for that is all there is of you."

"Most people buy not because they believe, but because the salesperson believes."

There are salesmen who reach The Game's pinnacle as GameBreakers. And there are icons: Ben Feldman. Ben was one of those individuals of such superior competence they define their profession. The ones you look at and think, "Yeah, that's the man I would like to be."

For his career with New York Life Ben was the epitome of his profession—the one who stood out from the herd like few had before, or have since. Like all GameBreakers Ben was a visionary.

He assessed, "What is the problem to be solved here?" He surveyed the field, determined where the high-potential opportunities were located, then constructed a bang-on solution to satisfy a most-probable customer group's needs.

Like Ben, the GameBreaker is someone everyone trusts. The impression is near universally favorable—open-minded, powerful work ethic, absolute commitment to getting better every day, intent on knowing a lot more than the competition. Things asked of him he can do faster and more to the point than others.

The approach applies directly to the prospect's need. In contrast the Pretender's question—*What will it take to close the deal?*—is patently sophomoric. Imagine the Pretender having the gumption to walk into a prospect's office unannounced and actually pull it off.

To a legendary figure like Ben Feldman, the process's outcome, and how the process is delivered, are equally important. Ben determined what was needed, then created a personal product of Olympic proportions, meeting the challenge for his customer/prospect's attention against an array of competing products.

He knew that what he was selling was not the actual product, but rather his approach to the sale process. The personal brand he created resulted from a monstrously effective approach to mastering The Game's nuances.

It may have come naturally to Ben Feldman, or it may have been learned. Either way, to the degree that something entailing so much grinding effort for most can be natural, Ben was a natural.

There is a lesson in Ben's success. It's easy to assume that Ben *had it* when he decided to make The Game his profession; doubt you would think so. He didn't look like Hollywood's version of a salesman, described as appearing more like a gnome, "short and stooped, pudgy and balding, with eyelids so droopy he appeared half asleep."

Deceptively bland, he was so shy he was reported to have once insisted on standing behind a screen when he spoke to an audience of fellow agents.

Ben didn't sound like a salesman. He wasn't slick; he didn't have a soothing, *no-problem,* Bill Clinton style. Rather, he spoke in declarative statements. He knew how to get to the point—neither too excessive, or intellectual, just convincing. People could sense his absolute belief in what was spoken.

He spoke softly, hesitantly, with a lisp. It was reported that, "sometimes he just sat there blinking and said nothing." But as he spoke he would lean forward, his rock-confident demeanor gathering them in. He was telling a story, his prospect in the starring role. Now there was rhythm in his hesitations. He would draw out his power phrases, then emphasize them with silence.

As support he would show a prospect his *textbook,* a loose-leaf binder containing financial histories of prominent men—Franklin D. Roosevelt for one—whose businesses or property had to be sold because they died with insufficient assets to pay estate taxes.

Taped inside the textbook's cover were a one thousand dollar bill and a few pennies. "For these," he would say, referring to the pennies, "you can get this"—the bill. He would have two checks printed especially for his client: one for a large sum to the Internal Revenue Service; a second for much less to New York Life. "You sign the little one today, we'll sign the big one."

Ben's belief in what he was doing never wavered. He saw a special opportunity, and seized it. He developed a unique perspective on his product's attributes, framed a compelling story, then proceeded to act as a true-believer. Each day, a masterpiece.

Success came no more overnight to Ben than anyone else who has taken on The Game as a profession. He just saw things differently, then developed a sale process so elegantly executed he made history. Ben Feldman wasn't perfect; he was just capable, reliable, willing, honest, and accountable. And he proved that anyone with the moxie to do it can sell like a tall person.

When he died at age 81 Ben stood above all as the world's greatest life-insurance salesman. Harry Hohn, New York Life's chairman, at

Ben's funeral suggested: "Ben really felt everyone in the world was under-insured, and he would do whatever it took to insure them."

It may take a while to develop your own notably competent personal product, but to the serious Game aspirant, time is no object; only the process of becoming matters.

If you're ready now, let's go. I'm going to do my best to show you how.

PART TWO

THE SALE PROCESS

CHAPTER FOUR

Sale-Process Components

How The Game Will Be Pursued

A natural order, determined by one of two viewpoints will dominate how The Game is pursued, as:

A competitive event, emphasizing outcomes; or

An experience, focused on personal-skills development as a continuing process.

Temperament—affecting personal preference—plays a role in which path this quest is likely to take, either approach capable of leading to Game success:

One is:	**The other:**
About feelings—focusing on gain, or loss—based on outcomes;	*Assumes developing effective actions will result in positive outcomes;*
About external reward—looking good: praise, acceptance, approval;	*Internal,* all about delivering quality of service;

Fickle, relying on outside factors for satisfaction;

Looks to process quality as its own reward;

About constant performance.

About constant improvement.

Treating The Game as a competitive event can be highly effective, but stressful .When viewed as a battle to be won, personal satisfaction or a sense of loss attaches to every transaction.

The experiential approach is not entirely stress-free, but the competitive need to perform moment-by-moment shifts to process quality, viewing results—negative or positive—as just part of the process. Mediocre results mean only adjustments are to be made.

And that defines an absolute: need for a formalized system defining the process. Importance isn't in the product being sold, or in the outcome. What *is* important is how the process looks, how it behaves, how it accomplishes what is intended, and its adaptability to the moment.

An orderly approach to a sale transaction tells your customer that you know what you are doing. A more random approach, relying on a lot of personalized delivery, will more likely only result in confusion, and unpredictability of outcomes.

The Sale Process

A sale is a singularity, outwardly similar in appearance to other sales, but always unique to itself. For that reason learning to participate in The Game is a hands-on experience. You have to do it to learn it.

Two dynamic entities participate: a salesman; and the circumstances. The circumstances are composed of a sale prospect, a pressing need, a product capable of fulfilling the need, the competitive environment, economic conditions, and sale venue.

The product to be sold holds certain definable characteristics, some important to one prospect, of lesser importance to another. Variations in the extent of need serve to segment the customer/prospect universe.

The salesman's great skill is in getting inside the other party's concerns in a disarming, simple, to-the-point manner. Quoting Vince Lombardi "Being brilliant on the basics" distinguishes these high-performance individuals.

A range of behavioral aspects combine to constitute the salesman's finished product. But one or two can elevate an inexperienced individual from moderately competent to very good, possibly to star status:

A well-informed understanding of a product's need-satisfying capabilities; creatively stated;

Ability to identify a particularly productive customer category, and identification of sale prospects with a clearly apparent need, and the means to act; and

Ability to develop a compelling sale presentation, definitively tailored to an individual customer's need.

Some appear to be genetically designed for The Game's particular needs; others have to work a little harder. For both, selling is a performance. It takes practice to perfect.

For the gifted individual, a natural inclination may be to shake any apple tree, and get as much fruit off it as possible, a talent defining a hereditary propensity for The Game. For most, talent of that sort is not natural, more often developed into a formalized system composed of two components: structure—what you do; and substance—how you do it.

A sale call is organized in the same workmanlike manner a fisherman prepares for a day at the trout stream. Preparation—who is to be contacted, what is to be discussed, and how it will be presented—establishes the basis for control. Sale prospects will remember when you made the extra effort to make what you had to say relevant to them. And when you didn't.

The sale process begins with lead generation—high-probability customer-prospect identification.

High-Probability Customers

Every product has a *most-probable* customer, a customer prospect holding recognizable need for your product, and the means to acquire it.

This customer-prospect category possesses the highest potential to contribute the most productive piece of a salesman's activity. It's common sense, like a farmer's search for which sheep make the best wool, to ferret this group out.

Customer prospects will be included within a reasonably recognizable population universe, whose occupants will range considerably in opportunity value. Not everyone you speak with will have the same potential, or view you or your company with the same affection.

Under a 1-10 rating, a 10 would be a near automatic sale; a rating of *one* would be *not-on-the-best-day-of-your-life*. Most high-potential prospects are going to fall within the 7-9 range, the *most probable* category, and will compose 80% of your production.

If your product is new, a certain group, *early adopters*, will be more immediately amenable to what you have to offer. In *Diffusion of Innovations*, Everett Rogers defined an early-adopter customer type as "an early customer of a company's product or technology." The term extended to include *lighthouse customers*, well-connected and influential individuals, particularly valuable as referral sources.

Early adopters like cutting-edge new things, and possess the wherewithal to acquire a new technology or service when first introduced. If they like something they can be quick to become lighthouse customers, aggressively recommending you or your product to others.

Beyond early adopters, customer prospects will range in degree of willingness to acquire your product. Some will need proof ("Who else is using the service?"), and some, testing the salesman's legendary persistence, will require several contacts before reaching a decision.

Of course there will be customers who will make the buying decision after the second, third, or fourth contact; others will require more determination to land. If eight contacts are required on-average to complete a sale, the math simplifies: eight contacts with the same individual to complete a sale is just a Game condition.

A Fish Fry—Or a Relaxing Day at the Trout Stream

Most activities dependent on developed skill in order to compete at a high level have their aphorisms: *You can schedule a fishing trip, but you can't schedule a fish fry*; and a day can be scheduled for sales calls. But scheduling a sale?

A fish fry assumes higher probability when the fisherman is determined to return home with a catch; when the fisherman's focus is on just an outing, a fish fry is considerably less probable. Success potential takes on real importance when the fisherman leaves with a commitment to return with fish.

One measures success by the experience—the other, the outcome. Was the result a creel full of fish? Or just a day at the trout stream? A similar condition applies to every sale transaction: as the fisherman is responsible for outcomes, so is the salesman.

The fisherman's first consideration is to go where the fish are, then to determine how the fish are best approached. Attention is given to time of day, location, weather conditions, current natural food supply—all important to catching (as opposed to entertaining) fish.

The fisherman changes locations and lures with some frequency, patiently working every stretch of promising water—whatever it takes to bring home the prize.

A fishing experience requires none of these. Time of day can be whenever it's convenient, using any lure available, and working whatever stretch of water is most easily accessed.

This individual, loosely described as a fisherman, may get lucky and catch a fish; every experienced fisherman admits to luck playing a part in fishing outcomes.

But the better prepared the fisherman, the more determined he is to involve every available advantage, the luckier he gets.

Substitute golf, football, marathon running, skiing, any activity requiring preparation to perform beyond mediocrity—The Game is no different. If a closed sale transaction isn't the focus, hope can only be that random luck will strike in the same manner that lightning is capable of doing.

A limited range of effort can provide the appearance of pursuing business activity. But the result can also be simply a feeling of having given it the old *college try*. Small comfort if the need to achieve extends beyond just the experience.

Raising the question, how is it some salespeople, the deal-closing ones—the kill or be killed ones—do particularly well, while others end up with nothing time after time? The answer is in how seriously the process has been taken.

When you are prepared, you know who you are going to speak with, how you will approach them, and what you intend to accomplish. The rest, like a coach's game plan, is simply execution.

CHAPTER FIVE

The Cold Call

Cold-call selling is rock-and-dirt country. The Game's serious pros reside here.

Cold-call success is a direct consequence of call-rate; there is no substitute for the number of calls made. For the neophyte salesman a few potential call-rate barriers may need to be addressed as each social style has its own potential inhibitors to Game participation.

Hesitancy, when assertive behavior is required, near universally results from fear: "The customer said he was happy;" "The owner won't see me;" "We're too expensive;" "Our prices are too high;" "They can't buy now."

Avoidance of prospecting, or closing a sale, results from irrational fears. No legitimate excuse is available for not making contacts with potential customers. A troublesome reason for insufficient call rate can result from an Amiable or Analytical style's cautious behavior.

An Amiable's need to be liked will conflict with an unavoidable potential of offending someone by an assertive action taken in a selling situation.

For the more analytically disposed a selling contact, prior to being completely prepared, may be difficult when the Analytical's preferences require having all the answers before exposure to possible ridicule, or worse, rejection.

A narrow behavioral comfort zone may hamper either style's ability to assume assertive behaviors needed when The Game is on.

More direct bottom-liner types—Drivers, and Expressives—can have their own self-created problems, possibly seeing themselves as *above it all*—too professional to deal with "unnecessary" concern for minutiae. Or they may feel that more detail-oriented Amiable and Analytical social styles are unable to appreciate the bottom-liner's assertive personality.

Regardless of social style, when it comes to a sales call, even the most well-adjusted can be subject to self-doubt, resulting from:

Fear of offending—The timid individual's fear of offending as a result of asserting a position directly contradicts the salesman's role—to force a conclusion, a function requiring assumption of a leadership role.

A need to be ultra-prepared—The Analytical's Achilles heel, no stone unturned, every question anticipated before discussion can begin. Here, *informed* can be confused with *perfection*.

An over-developed self-image—*If they need me, they will call.* Above-it-all self-importance pre-empts good sense. A weak way of avoiding rejection—or making sales.

Attaching risk to every call—*Why would I bother calling them, they'll just turn me down.* The mind made up; behavior reflecting the position. A presentation expecting rejection will be half-hearted; fear of failure imposing a self-fulfilling prophecy.

Unwillingness to ask for referrals—*I don't need anyone's help. I can do it myself.* After having done good work for someone, avoiding asking for referrals, afraid those parties will feel exploited or offended, an opportunity has just closed.

Being secretly ashamed of being a salesperson—If you aren't satisfied with the salesman's role, how can you possibly convince yourself to acquire a salesman's needed behaviors?

Fear of rejection—The salesman's deadliest obstacle: fear of the word *no*. In extreme, loathed.

Mind-Theory's Role in Presentation Quality

Everyone experiences occasional insecurity. Sometimes feelings are small, at other times formidable.

But regardless of size, allowing insecurity to control your approach to a sale transaction will result in being rendered less effective. And that leads to *mind-theory*, a frequently experienced, self-caused, destructive bump in this road.

Mind-theory results from fear of rejection. It's not unusual for an inexperienced salesman to behave in an awkward manner when acting on what is presumed will expose them to hostility, resorting to *figuring the other person out*.

A self-defined opinion of how the salesman would feel, *if pushed*, and the resulting assumption that *this is how the other must feel*, is destructive. When conditions call for assertive actions, the *I know how I would feel if pushed*, emotion rushes in, rendering the salesman a eunuch.

Sympathizing with someone else's feelings requires knowing what's inside their head. It hasn't been successfully done before, and is not likely to be done now. Mind-theory has no place in The Game—ever.

CHAPTER SIX

A Unique Selling System

It's possible for ordinary people to do extraordinary things. But to do that, a system—an organized way of doing things—is essential.

Like any of several roles played every day it's common sense to perform the role as it should be played. When you're a friend, live the moment as a friend; as a father, live the moment as a father; and when you are a salesman, live the moment as a salesman lives the moment.

The role played is as an actor in a highly conspicuous drama. Coming across as an organized, competent individual sets a tone. Just prior to making a telephone call—or initiating a face-to-face call—the role is assumed.

Do you approach a sale as though the world was coming to an end? Of course you do. And why wouldn't you? In a competitive world the advantage you gain from being even marginally more energetic, alert, and attractive can be the edge that gets the sale. You can make excuses or make sales. You can't do both.

Preparation for a business call includes searching out: what does the prospect do? How important is the prospect's company to the industry? Where is their pressing need? What products of similar type to yours do they currently use?

The discovery process can be simple, or have an aura of espionage. Under either, pre-call preparation is required for a day spent at The Game to be more than just an outing. The challenge is to make the premise simple and elegant, to make it realistic and compelling.

When you understand the objective, and the prospect doesn't, the presentation is your show. Like an actor slipping into character prior to stepping onto a stage, the salesman, acting in the lead role, draws the prospect into the essential elements of a good story.

The experienced salesman knows every nuance of a presentation in the manner a professional football coach's game plan anticipates what Sunday's opponent is likely to throw at them. And, like an NFL game plan, not every selling proposal attaches the same strategy.

A strong selling presentation requires a position to be taken—a firm, unequivocal statement. There are the facts of the story, reinforced by the eloquence of the narrative. It can:

Be purely rational, just the facts;

Focus on a strictly emotional appeal; or

Combine the two.

Leaving the Pretenders to contemplate their consistently ineffective results, very effective selling is creative; most definitely appealing to the emotions—an artfully framed position, supported by one or two relevant facts.

Decisions are seldom made for purely rational, or purely emotional, reasons. A little rationale goes a long way; pure emotion taken alone applies most effectively when there are life-and-death, small children, or love-life improvement possibilities.

The Pretender's fact-based data-dump delivery of a product's attributes, or the purely emotional approach—*forget-the-facts, let's-just-do-this-on-the-fly*—are pure improvisations, random charges into the fray. Both are Game equivalents to a street musician playing the air guitar.

A Unique Selling Proposition—Framing

A variety of factors define how we see things; how we go about life.

For that reason every product attaches a *unique selling proposition*—a compelling statement of differentiation illustrating the product's attributes. A unique selling proposition may be an old idea, viewed from a different perspective, or a new creative idea.

Either communicates a verbal illustration of how the product solves a need. Psychologists refer to the act as the *framing effect*.

Framing defines variations in how the same information is presented: expensive/high quality? Price/value? Save time? Save money? … Imaginative framing is the most effective driver behind positive sale-transaction outcomes.

Framing explains why ground beef labeled, "85% lean," will sell more ground beef than the same package labeled, "15% fat." A surgery's "80% survival rate" sounds less unsettling than "20% mortality."

While competitors resort to promoting their personal credentials as a selling point, or worse, tearing down their competition, place attention on your product's needs-satisfying qualities. Then frame them with a creative statement illustrating why a prospect should be moved to action.

Ben Feldman's life insurance was framed by comfort—"your family will be taken care of." "When you walk out, the money walks in." "Let us write the big check; you write the small one."

Selling Presentation Dynamics

The simple pursuit of a prospect for purposes of doing business with them is what the competition is doing.

Before pursuing a working relationship on a first call, it's reasonable to objectively consider that a prospect likely doesn't care about the individual making the proposal, his business, or whether he is successful.

A salesman is a stage manager, setting the tone for a selling event, initiating the action, and setting the pace. There is no end to ways available to achieve the desired result.

For all, a sale is engaged, or lost, during the *golden three,* a sales call's first three minutes when, like an accomplished coach's game-plan execution, sale-call steering determines the prospect's:

Social Style—how this individual most probably prefers to be dealt with. Are they a bottom-liner, requiring you get straight to the point? Or do they need to spend time on the preliminaries? Feel the merchandise? Ask some questions?

Perceptions—a prospect will have preconceived ideas, potentially at odds with the facts of what you have to offer, and how they view you, your product, and your company. With perceptions addressed, discussion moves on—to need.

Needs—what pressing need does the product address? If the prospect operates a business, needs evaluation may address how the business is promoted, how many salespeople are in the organization, how do they develop new business, or support existing customers?

If the prospect is a senior company employee, their most pressing need may include being made to look good—or to avoid looking bad.

Personal needs can apply to family protection, looking good, or avoidance of looking bad. But, whether the need is business or personal, all needs are practical and equally compelling.

With the preliminaries determined, the presentation's narrative proceeds to weave in relevant details, the telling supported by:

Having your story straight—every word framed into the simplest structure;

Your personal voice—delivered as a conversation between acquaintances. To the point; spoken easily and naturally;

Word choice—precise colorful language; sprinkled with a few power phrases—short on adjectives and adverbs;

Rhythm—a cadence, a flow. The narrative slows, speeds up, pauses, kept on point, and interesting; and

Conventions—speech and grammar, correct; the prospect extended the full courtesy of understanding their position. To sell your thoughts you are *on*. Edgy, but not nervous.

When Your Meeting Is Face-to-Face

Use Eye Contact. Within limits. About half a face-to-face interaction needs direct eye contact. Much less and you will appear unsure of yourself; more, and the appearance will be coming on too strong.

Offer a Firm Handshake. Firm. Not a Force-10 bone crusher, or a limp-wristed dead fish. Either extreme risks a negative first impression.

Smile. If you're not in the mood, fake it. Show some teeth. You, and the person you are meeting, will feel better.

When the Sale Call Is by Telephone

Avoid the clichéd opening line, *"How are you today?"* It comes across as shallow.

Under Either Format

Begin with an engaging question: what prospect activities can you help? If a question doesn't gain traction, begin with a statement: the main idea.

Ben Feldman had no problem with being straightforward, "You're already broke, and you don't know it." Of course Ben's gravitas was useful in pulling off such a potentially inflammatory statement. He was fully wired to comprehend a statement's value in determining the presentation's direction.

Whether the transaction is by telephone, or face-to-face, determine the prospect's social style by encouraging them to speak. Having done that you can anticipate what you are getting into, and what action you will take. It's in the story.

The story transforms a transaction from just a casual outing into a memorable event.

Presentation Narrative—the Story

Like music or well-written literature, a presentation has form and structure. And, in that sense, relies on a certain amount of theater.

In music, noise converts into something pleasant to the ear; vivid word pictures in literature hold the reader's attention. The same applies to a selling presentation's narrative; knowledge is best remembered through a good story.

The best salesmen have often achieved their status because they are very good at slinging a great story. There is good reason. Film director Alfred Hitchcock placed a story into perspective—"A good story is life with the dull parts taken out." Nothing more needs saying as applies to selling.

In its classic form, a story narrative introduces two characters. In this particular event, the salesman and the prospect. The salesman plays an authority figure, possessing a certain charisma, personal skills, or expert knowledge required to overcome a prospect's near inevitable skepticism.

Your prospect is a character in the story. He has an objective. A want. Desire. A need. The prospect's objective—solving a pressing need—is the presentation's driving force.

What distinguishes a story from other kinds of communications is a certain kind of structure. A story doesn't need to be unique. Stories more probably work best when they reference other stories.

The test of a presentation's quality is, if the prospect understood what was said, did they believe it? If they believed it, did they remember the key points? A creatively framed narrative provides context—*why* a point matters.

The best stories are guides to action—cues and reference points stressing something important. Sometimes a story may fall short, the outcome failing to perform its intended role; changes in conditions require occasional story-content revision.

Absent a story, a presentation is more probably a collection of random statements, or a data dump of information. Neither likely to be remembered.

What is said is not at issue; what is *heard*, based on how what was said, is most definitely the issue. An iPad with a few bullet points can't do that.

The Compelling Presentation

Is a sale within reach every time you initiate a sale call? You surely should pursue it as though it were.

Selling styles will have differences, some distinctive. But powers of observation, assertiveness, the ability to read people's nonverbal communication, and a not-to-be-denied attitude, are common to experienced salesmen.

A selling presentation isn't a sermon. A windy lecture is incapable of presenting a gripping reason for action. The best sales presentations don't sound like presentations. A good selling presentation may hit a few poetic notes, but discards fancy words. A persuasive proposition doesn't require an ability to dazzle, just to make the point persuasively.

As applies to most activities there are many ways of getting things done. The concept applies particularly well to selling. Original selling ideas and concepts are the work of creative individuals. What makes a style persuasive is not entirely straightforward—different isn't always better, but better is always different.

What motivates someone to act in the manner you want them to act? It's in the answer to the question, *what's in it for me?*

We know it when we see it. As example, Ben Feldman's power phrases were sometimes subtle; other times, hard-hitting; always capable of dominating a presentation. His creative phrasing tapped into emotions, stimulating a clear understanding, and retention, of his presentation's main idea.

A really good narrative is the heart of a presentation. Stories are woven into the presentation's fabric, making the main idea compelling. The story's language, even understated, is clear—the result, effective.

It's in how the main idea is expressed. A fresh approach to making a point in a way not quite like anything seen before is conceptually attractive. But, for more immediate sense to be made, attaching similarity to a prospect's stored feelings or knowledge can considerably increase memorability.

If power phrases are not a normal part of your communication, adding that expertise will play a significant role in developing an effective selling style.

Buying decisions aren't typically a result of a well-considered cost/benefit analysis. Rather, they are more emotional—outsourced to feelings. *It just feels right.*

Compelling delivery makes people want to agree; it's about energy, enthusiasm, charm, likeability, product knowledge, knowledge of the prospect's pressing need ... Certain consistencies are uniform to compelling presentations:

There is a motivational point. A selling presentation requires a firm position taken. The prospect *needs* this service because: they will secure more business leads, reduce time spent organizing, stand out from the competition, reduce their costs, make their activities more productive, look better, protect their family ...;

The prospect is actively involved. The more memorable the connection between the prospect and the product, the more positive will be the outcome;

When the prospect asks for a specific product capability, show them. In context with their need;

Things are kept moving, efficiently, not rushed. Moving too fast will not allow the prospect to connect; too slow and attention span will be lost;

The meaning of what is being demonstrated is made clear. Request feedback. Confirm that they understand why your product so effectively addresses their need;

Use illustrations. Pictures sell—pretty pictures, even better. "A picture is worth a thousand words." The illustration can be visual, or spoken as a power phrase;

57

When the price argument is raised, go to the value discussion—avoid price justification. Instead, "If you need a sledge hammer for the job, a tack hammer at any price is still only a tack hammer." "You have a moving job, a bicycle won't solve your problem."

Skilled activities have in common structure, a logical process. A sale presentation transitions through three distinct stages:

Engagement;

A well-supported, clearly illustrated, premise, the presentation's main idea; and

The Close

Arriving at an understanding of why structure works is freeing. Master the principles, and you are then at liberty to add your own personal touches.

A more complex sale process may require two closes: the first, a presentation appointment; the second, the solutions presentation, demonstrating how a pressing need will be solved. With either, a convincing presentation is:

Plausible—limited to one or two salient facts supporting need satisfaction; and

Persuasive—a touch of theater, capable of bringing even Sinclair Lewis's Elmer Gantry out of his chair.

Experienced salesmen combine the elements of craftsman and showman, engaging the prospect, addressing what may have been incorrect perceptions.

At any storyteller's disposal are elements common to great communicators:

A favorable initial impression;

A projection of confidence, bordering on, but not crossing over to, arrogance;
An empathetic attitude;
A structured delivery; and
A dynamic close.

Sale structure is about timing—where the next particular elements go, and how much attention to give to each. Time between making the point, and closing the sale, is necessarily of short duration. A prospect will have mentally checked out at something between the 10 and 15-minute mark.

The neuroscientific community hasn't given definition to what happens to make the curtain drop so predictably. But, at that point, the brain hits the *pause* button, underscoring a sale presentation imperative: at 10-to-15 minutes reengage, close the sale, or vacate the field.

CHAPTER SEVEN

The Sale Process

Sale-Transaction Communication

A selling presentation is unique—of the imagination—one creative intelligence interacting with another. Engaging the other involves listening, paying attention to what is felt about the goings-on from the other side of the table. They probably mean something.

The personal flavoring rounding out a sale presentation derives from a few personal characteristics common to notably competent Game participants:

Confidence—a huge spirit holds an unbeatable advantage. You are convinced your proposal will be a triumph for the prospect. Confidence supports high performance.

Attitude—time to close the sale? Let it rip! You can't control how things go, but you absolutely can control the transaction's direction, and your responses. An assumptive close asks, "How shall we go about this?" *Whether* has no place in the discussion.

An indomitable will—you may not close them all, but pursue them as though you expect to.

Enthusiasm—Yes, definitely. Show some enthusiasm. Just don't be foolish about it. A cheerleader's style isn't necessary. Charging into the fray with wild abandon is too extreme for most. But a blasé approach is selling's black-hole equivalent.

Communication experts generally maintain 65% of communicated information—tone of voice, facial expressions, and an array of body language components—is nonverbal; voice provides 30%, the remaining five percent consists of words spoken.

Taking full advantage, focus presentation communication to:

Illustrate unequivocal belief in your statements.

Radiate a confident, enthusiastic manner—your feelings for what your service will do for your prospect will result in their reflecting that enthusiasm. Convincing people to work with you is in considerable part determined by attitude. If you believe they should, so will they.

Illustrate full command of product knowledge—questions receiving to-the-point responses.

Engage the prospect memorably—a prospect will reflect your manner. If you can't warm up ahead of time, warm yourself up while building a case for your product.

Connect directly with the prospect's need—how your product will make their life better, save them money, make them look better, make them more efficient …

Get into what you know; forget guarding what you don't know—absolute product knowledge mastery isn't necessary. A few questions requiring follow-up can represent opportunity.

Open up—and lighten up. A relaxed, open demeanor is an advantage. The role played, that of a leader. You know what your prospect needs to do, where they need to go, and how to get there.

The other end of the style scale, a closed ultra-cool demeanor, may appear thoughtful or deep. But an aloof appearance may just as well communicate boredom, even arrogance. Stay loose. You can be cool later when impressing someone at the herd's after 5:00 watering hole is the objective.

Be complimentary—a little flattery goes a long way; people enjoy a little ego stroking. Just don't overdo it. *Nice shoes*, no; *I admire the reputation you (or your company) have achieved*, yes.

Avoid using a prospect's name as a bludgeon—speaking a prospect's name once or twice in a discussion is sensible; overplaying the name makes you sound like one of selling's favorite clichés: the *please, please like me* school of everyone's genuinely shallow individual.

Pay attention to your nonverbal language—lean toward your prospect when they speak; nod to acknowledge your understanding of what is said. If you are on the telephone lean forward, even if the person on the other end of the line can't see you; acknowledge their points ("Yes," "I understand," "Good …"). Use feedback to confirm you understand their concerns.

Respect resistance—an objection means, *I'm thinking*. Balking on a point may simply be a request to be sold.

Mental Preparation—Just Before the Call

Consciously or not a prospect subject to your selling presentation will be asking:

What is this about?

Why should I care?

Why should I keep listening?

Prepare to perform, referencing:

Your Mindset—enthusiastic? Apathetic? Fearful? Enthusiastic is the only acceptable viewpoint. A few written descriptive adjectives for reference—*competent, professional, credible, trustworthy, composed, enthusiastic*—are useful. If defensive thoughts creep into your feelings, the image you defined will keep your mindset on track.

In the process, avoid:

Badmouthing the competition	Arguing
Showing irritation	Flippant remarks
Weak communication—words, or nonverbal	Backpedaling

What you expect to accomplish—is the intent to set a solutions presentation appointment? Or is the objective to close a sale?

The First Impression to Be Made

Your prospect's antennae are picking up a full array of impressions. You appear to them as confident or insecure, knowledgeable or naïve, trusting or suspicious. The conclusion reached is instantaneous and, for the moment, final. Without your consent others make snap judgments, potentially forming lasting impressions about you.

A first impression's potential impact promotes, or detracts from, your objective. A changed opinion may result later, but people attach a not easy-to-replace image to first impressions.

The stereotypical salesman is characterized as an aggressive, dynamic, outgoing type associated with Driver and Expressive styles. But, to an Amiable or Analytical style, bottom-liner stereotypical behavior holds the very real prospect of being a serious put-off.

For that reason, first-time contact is not macho, overly friendly, or particularly analytical. A neutral manner tunes into a prospect's wavelength, before proceeding.

Stated in a straightforward friendly style, like someone sitting on the front stoop talking to a friend, a sale presentation relies on a balance between emotional input and rational analysis, neither trumping the other. Salesmen who get too emotionally worked up, or who attempt to rely on logic alone, tend to make dramatic sale-process errors.

The salesman has to deliver, requiring a healthy dose of confidence laced with attitude. For bottom-liners, get to the point; if an Analytical prefers some detail, no problem; when an Amiable is friendly and chatty, so are you. The object: engage them. As they prefer to be engaged.

Presentation Structure

Sale transactions apply a sequence of ritual.

The sale process is orderly. A presentation's structure unfolds in three acts: a beginning, middle, and end, all framed about a main idea.

The main idea deserves emphasis: there is one main idea, only one. Identify it. Express it creatively, forcefully landing on it. The transaction applies a sequence, keeping things simple, and connected. The best salesmen may not follow every rule every time, but it's better to learn the rules before breaking them.

In setting a solutions presentation appointment, the activity is relatively simple. The more complex solutions presentation follows the same independent steps, each acting interdependently with the others:

First Stage—Determine Your Prospect's Social Style

Actively observe the other person's behavior, speaking only to initiate the discussion: *Good morning, I am here (I am calling) because ... What will be of interest to you?* Then, let them speak. Within the first 30 seconds inside a presentation's golden three minutes, the prospect's personal style is determined

Was a lot of open emotional expression exhibited? Or was demeanor more businesslike? Did they ask for facts? Did they want to know about you, or your company? Did they cut straight to the point, "What do you have that will be of interest to me?"

An individual's tendencies—to the point, or preferring a little sensitivity—considerably influence probable response. With your part of the discussion formatted to make them feel comfortable, they will more likely be open to what you have to say.

With determination of how this individual most likely prefers to be approached, remain on-point as perceptions about your company, or product, and the need to be addressed are determined.

Second Stage—Determine Your Prospect's Perceptions

Prospects will have certain perceptions—preconceived opinions and viewpoints—possibly influencing their acceptance of your proposal.

Perceptions are assumed reality. Are you seen only as a salesman? The bearer of an opportunity? Is your product seen as just another lookalike? Have they been approached before by a competitor or one of your company's representatives, but were unimpressed? Do they see your product as too expensive for too little value? Do they already have a product or service they see as being as good as yours?

A prevalent preconception is expectation of intent to coerce them into spending money on something they *probably don't need,* and *isn't in the budget anyway*. Not all, but some, contacts will be openly receptive to what you have to say. Such times are gifts. Success with the rest may require the gut-level effort that keeps The Game so interesting.

A prospect's mind open to your premise will have dismissed preconceived notions as having no relevance.

Third Stage—Determining Need

One essential condition is capable of exciting a prospect: how a product will solve their pressing need.

Need disclosure can begin with a question: "How are you doing it now?" Or a statement: "You have a problem, I can solve it." When you ask your prospect to participate and receive resistance, without hesitation, move on.

Some Game mistakes are packaged in industrial strength, the ultimate, beginning a presentation before determining need. Need determination is a binding requirement for most professions. In medicine, determine the problem before prescribing; law, the same. Where to dig? Football strategy? What is the prospect's pressing need your product is uniquely capable of filling?

If your product is new to them, will what you have represent an improvement? Will it solve a problem? Will they be better off for it? Who do they sell to? How do they market their service? How do they pursue new business? Do they need more business contacts? Or is the need more personal? Do they have a need to impress? Is their need to avoid looking bad? Is the need to protect their family?

Some needs are objective—more business leads at less cost, more efficient sales organization usage, higher productivity. Others, more personal. The personal-needs category may require some effort to identify. But personal needs' influence can be just as formidable as more apparent business-improvement needs.

Among notable *must-have* personal needs are:

Desire to win—*"An edge over the competition? I want it!"*
Members of this group are often early adopters; frequently market leaders.

Desire to look good—*"Of course I appreciate acknowledgment, more particularly from the guy who signs my paycheck."*
Anyone whose role is to generate business for their company can be motivated by the opportunity to look good. This prospect will document reasons for their decision to the fullest extent possible. Your part—lay out a convincing story.

Desire to be admired—your prospect's ego will be heard. Focus placed on the decision's appearance first; product value as a distant second. A very real concern can be a desire to be seen as shrewd.

Avoidance of looking bad—one can be as concerned with not making a mistake as another is with having made a good decision. One plays to win; the other, not to lose.

Whatever the basis, needs are practical. And whether objective or subjective, one or two will dominate.

Fourth Stage—Engagement

Now, three minutes into the discussion, with the prospect fully engaged, the curtain rises. Lights! Action! The nervous system, fully involved. Demeanor, edgy. No appearance of nervousness.

Adding a personalized element, your prospect's mind's-eye now becomes involved. Beyond processing information, they feel it. Dramatic main-idea framing will be remembered. Without need to force a point of view, the prospect's interest is addressed conversationally. No appearance of aggressiveness.

Nearly every "how-to" selling book of note has acknowledged questions as among the selling kit's most powerful tools:

At the knowledge (left-brain) level—was what was said understood?

At the feeling (right-brain) level—how was their nonverbal response expressed? Interested? Tense? Skeptical? Enthusiastic? Hesitant? Your message:"Did I hear you correctly?"

The sale process's defining moment has been reached—the close. "We *need* this product." Now act on it.

Fifth Stage—the Close

Contrary to frequent mind-theory assumptions, assertive action to force a decision doesn't make you disagreeable. You are simply supporting what you have determined is your customer's best decision.

Two options apply to a close—direct or finesse—both effective. One, in-your-face; the other, indirect.

Direct—a direct close gets to the point: "The 1700 model is your best option, it's going to change how you do things." "It appears a one-million-dollar policy will cover your needs."

Finesse—the indirect close, just as definite, involves the customer with an open-ended question: "Which model will fill your long-term needs best?" "What day is best for delivery?" "How many will be required to satisfy your needs?"

Selling pros know when the moment arrives, and, without hesitation, close the sale. Fear of rejection is set aside for a common-sense determination: *what is needed here?* The salesman's role is unequivocal: absolute certainty of intent, urgency, energy, enthusiasm, assertiveness.

The form of close dependent on intent:

Setting an appointment to present your product?; or

Presenting a product's need-satisfying qualities to a qualified prospect?

Any of selling's acknowledged most effective closes can be effective:

Assumptive Close—the only decision: How much? Or, when? The assumptive close is a statement: "This is going to change the way you do things." "The 1400 model will serve your needs best." "We'll schedule Friday for delivery."

Alternate of Choice—an assumptive-close version, the alternate of choice asks a question: "Is delivery tomorrow, or the next day, better for you?" Followed by: "Morning, or afternoon?" Then: "10:00, or 11:00?"

An alternative can be: "Which model will work best—A, or, B?"

Takeaway—most effective when, following a series of attempts, efforts have not resulted in a positive response. Your decision is: "Okay, this is the best we're going to get, let's do something." The response: "Apparently our service isn't for you. If circumstances change I will be happy to follow up with you." Or, a statement: "We're not for everyone." Followed by a polite "Thank you for the discussion."

To enable any:

Ask a question—open-ended; avoid closed-ended ("yes," or "no") questions:

"What is our next step?"

"What would you like from me to complete the process?"

"Which model will support your activities best?"

"Who else will be involved in the decision?"

Make a statement

"The mid-range model seems your best choice."

"This places a considerably improved horse in your race."

"With our support you will maintain your business activity with fewer salespeople, or your current salesforce will raise the bar."

"We will save you time, or the time you spend will be more effective."

Ben Feldman would say "You write the small check; we'll write the big one."

Then … silence. Avoid the urge to speak when response to your silence is their silence. Silence communicates thought being given; momentum is in your favor. A pre-emptive comment holds high potential for triggering *no*. They will eventually speak. And when they do, probability favors your position.

The Counterfeit Presentation

Sale-call problems result not so much from how something is said, more likely it's the superficiality resulting from lack of preparation.

The professional salesman's process is precise. Not so the Pretender's counterfeit versions: data-dump, or random. Both versions are so prevalent they have achieved cliché status. To The Game, what paint-by-numbers is to art.

Next to the use of stale phrases, the worst cancers in selling are the data dump, and the breezy random approach to a sale presentation.

Pretend selling is easy. It's preachy, no point needed; accomplished amateurs know how it's done. It's in the emotions. The Pretender makes use of hyperbole ("This product will double your sales.") and attempts to ingratiate the prospect, the presentation supported by regurgitation of memorized facts. Pretend sales calls seldom result in a closed sale.

What makes a pretend presentation not really a presentation? How many of a few really choice faux pas are woven into the delivery? Just:

Make a prospect wonder why they need to be speaking with you at all.

Begin with a summary of who you are, and what you do. Preferably in a breathless delivery, attempting to avoid dismissal before launching into product facts.

Ignore their comments.

Stay with your line of thought. Tell them about your product. Questions can be answered when you're finished.

Use as many facts as you can.

The data dump at its pinnacle. Leave the prospect reeling from the depth of technical knowledge you bring to the event.

Don't be afraid to exaggerate your product's attributes.

A little hyperbole adds spice. Who wouldn't want to increase their sales by 20% in the first month?

Make clear your preconceived knowledge of their business.

They will comment on anything that doesn't seem right.

Speak in a perfectly controlled voice, preferably in a way-cool monotone.

The communicated lack of enthusiasm will strip an already dull presentation's content with the masterful touch of a lecture on botanical evolution.

Don't bother to close with some premise for a next step.

"If they want it, they will say so."

A counterfeit sale's components go together something like this:

Preparation

Good enough is, good enough.

Presentation

The Pretender proceeds to The Game's most unforgiving faux pas, a directionless, hot-air-filled data-dump, or a series of random thoughts. Both ending in embarrassment.

Lack of substance confirms a prospect's natural predisposition—assumption that a salesman's only interest is to impose something on them they don't need, can't afford, and wants to take time they don't have.

The Close

The Pretender never quite comes to a conclusion. He just hopes the other party will somehow see the light, and respond. In communicating what should be a definite statement—a sale close—the Pretender never gets to the point. A direct attempt to close? Too risky; they might say no.

Follow-up

"They said they would call if they were interested."

By nature the Pretender's too-often apparent strategy is to deceive, or centers on hope that the prospect may be bored into submission. But more probably they will simply give up on getting straight answers.

From a prospect's perspective, antagonism is a natural result when pretend selling resorts to gimmicks and noise to make the sale. More particularly objectionable is the whole thing amounts to truly bad selling.

What the counterfeit presentation offers in terms of emotional satisfaction—the problem solved, questions answered—is complete lack of density. No resonance. No sense of accomplishment. At a more profound level it's an expression of disrespect, and an apparently aggressive lack of concern.

Real selling is difficult, a high-wire act with no net. Serious preparation determines the prospect's probable need, how the prospect likely will prefer to be sold, and how the presentation will be framed to memorably communicate how the need will be satisfied.

The Solutions-Presentation Appointment

Prospect identified, main idea framed, the gist of the presentation set, The Game begins: a direct cold call, a letter describing your answer to their pressing need, a telephone call, or email requesting an appointment. Email being the least effective; the direct cold call the preferred standard.

If Your Approach Is By Email

When the introduction is by email, treat it like a letter. Have a greeting, a body, and a closing. Leave out text-message lingo like emoticons and abbreviations. The result will tell the person you are contacting that a little more time and thought were given before writing this.

If Your Approach Is By Telephone

You are calling because you:

Just wanted to introduce yourself?

Were wondering how they are doing today?

Have a product you would like to show them? Or …

Have a product that will solve their pressing need, and that—***they must see.***

Stating the obvious, the *what's-in-it-for-me* premise is a slam-dunk equivalent.

If Your Preference Is a Letter

A letter can be sent prior to, or following, telephone contact, stating what the discussion will mean to the prospect.

Good written selling communication gets results by presenting the case in the simplest way possible, paralleling the way you speak, sounding as though you were conversing directly with your prospect, stating:

Your purpose—why you are writing to them;

Your meaning—specific;

The tone—positive and confident. Active voice used. Professional, but informal;

The message—easily understood; and

A call for action—what you want them to do, or what they can expect from you.

You will naturally follow whatever writing format was learned through training or experience. But writing form evolves; a format deemed contemporary five years ago can appear dated today.

It isn't necessary to become an advertising copywriter to be capable at written business communication, but the copywriter's process is little different from a business communications writer. In both, the objective is to create a call for action.

Good business-letter writing is succinct, no wasted words. A sales letter is limited to one or two key points supporting how your product will solve a pressing need.

Unlike a newsy personal letter to an old friend, a sales letter, read aloud, probably will sound stiff. The distinction is the sales letter addresses the same careful thought applied to a magazine print ad costing thousands of dollars to place.

Why should they read your letter? A good idea badly expressed can sound like a bad idea. Before writing anything, think through your strategy.

The sales letter combines three elements:

The opening paragraph—*this letter is written to you because ...* the reason for the letter. The reader will be engaged, or the letter will be dismissed as of no interest;

Support—how your product will deliver on the premise stated. Between the opening and closing paragraphs, main-idea support is relevant and concise. No fifty-cent words, just to-the-point, *this-is-what-we-will-do-for-you* language;

The closing paragraph—a call for action. Short. To the point. Dynamic. You have supported why the prospect needs your product. Now state your follow-up intent, or ask them to respond.

Word, sentence, or document length is no less compelling whether short, or long. But "short words are best" is advice ascribed to Winston Churchill, who finished with "and old words when short are best of all."

A sales letter's structure includes some potential open manholes to avoid:

Long paragraphs—they are not read. In contrast with a literary work, reduce business letter paragraphs to two sentences;

Passive language—adjectives and adverbs weaken written communication;

Thought tangents—these shift relevance to thoughts other than prospect need *(It may be of interest to you to know that ...);*

Editorializing—*(I really believe this is right for you ...)* illustrates lack of confidence;

Glittering generalities—(outstanding, fabulous, awesome, break-through …);

Excessively formal phrasing—terms not used in every day speech *(share, if you will, thus)*.

A few clichéd examples are worth noting:

Needless to say—an expression which is, *needless to say*.

Enclosed herewith, or please find—stilted hyperbole.

As you know; as per our conversation; as you are well aware …

I am writing this letter to inform you that …

Please rest assured.

For your perusal, review, and consideration—is the intent to sound like your letter originated in the 1920s?

If you have any further questions, please do not hesitate to contact me—seriously? You wouldn't actually say that. Would you?

I would like to take this opportunity to … Just say it: thank you.

More than happy to … how achieved?

All, every, never … overcompensating.

We hope—no better way to show lack of confidence.

Perhaps—tentative.

Attached please find—superfluous. The reader will find it.

You can say much of what you want to say with word pictures: metaphors, similes, and epigrams. You get their drift; they can make your recipient want to read on.

For a business letter, only perfect spelling, grammar, and sentence structure is *good enough*. Before finalizing, verify that what is expressed, and how it's stated, is motivating. If not, rewrite it, write it again—seven, eight, nine, ten times if required—to get it right.

The Solutions Presentation

You have established that your main idea addresses:

Improving the prospect's business;

Making them more effective, more accomplished in less time;

Making them look better, or avoid looking bad;

Protecting their family;

Making their work easier; or

Providing a competitive advantage.

The main idea is supported by the:

Telling of the story—a word picture, framing how the product satisfies a pressing need; and

Relevant facts—complex ideas, simplified; simple ideas kept simple. Get too caught up in production of information and your prospect will drown in the data.

Condense your product's value to one or two salient points directly addressing the prospect's need, as expressed in the main idea. Overloading your prospect with more information only complicates making a decision.

Word pictures ("This service is like having a Ferrari in your driveway." "When you walk out, the money walks in.") make meaning clear: a selling proposition at its most elegant, simply stated.

CHAPTER EIGHT

Engaging Long-Term Memory of the Main Idea

Sale presentation success depends on several factors, one stands above all—how the main idea is understood, and remembered.

Activating your prospect's long-term memory of what the presentation means to them relies on an understanding of how memory works. The memory database serves two primary functions:

As a fund of stored knowledge; and

As a reference to assess future experiences.

The right-brain efficiently remembers the gist of a lifetime of experiences. Relating a product to a prospect's past positive experience, or relevant recent experience, can greatly improve main idea recall.

Short-term, or *working*, memory is the brain's *scratch-pad* where just-acquired information is processed. Alan Baddeley, a British researcher most associated with characterizing working memory, describes working-memory components as including:

Auditory, the spoken word;

Visual, what is seen; and

Executive, a controlling function, keeping track of activities engaged by working memory components.

Converting short-duration memory into longer-term memory relies on emotional involvement. Relatively simple modifications to a presentation's structure can effectively stick a point:

Include visual support—cognitive psychologist Richard Mayer, noted for experiments in how information delivered is subsequently recalled, tested three groups: one receiving information by hearing; another through sight; and a third group combining both senses. The third group won hands down. Multi-sensory exposure resulted in more accurate, longer-lasting, recall.

Taken alone, visual processing trumps hearing when hearing is taken alone. But visual processing doesn't just assist in remembering—it dominates.

Multi-sensory learning further deals with a highly counter-intuitive property: more is better. Logically, it might seem otherwise, but not so. Main-idea support, when complex, improves retention.

Make the presentation's support elaborate—a short-term memory can be made long-term by a form of recall referred to as *elaborative rehearsal.*

Elaborative rehearsal relates new information to stored information. Power phrases, metaphors, similes, and epigrams, directly related to the prospect assist in encoding a memory.

The more formidable the impression at the moment of learning ("you're already broke, and don't know it") the more readily the information will be recalled.

Reference examples—examples make use of other's experiences. If a high-profile individual has had a similar experience, or a large number of people have had similar results, the memory is more likely to be retained.

Vividly frame the main idea—dramatic illustrations can have profound effects on memory. It isn't enough to state the difference. Stark contrast will more likely be remembered. The more vivid the framing, the more completely the main idea will be retained.

Ben Feldman, a master at framing, placed a positive spin on his presentation's main idea. Ben's life-insurance presentations never mentioned death as a prerequisite for making good on the product. He sold comfort, and cheap money: "When you walk out, we walk in;" "I do not sell insurance, I sell money. I sell dollars for pennies apiece. My dollars cost three cents per dollar, per year."

Competitive insurance salesmen emphasized a different thought—life insurance as a savings vehicle, or investment.

Employ contrast—*I've seen this before.* It isn't enough to state the difference. There must be the force of contrast to remember. Contrast appeals to a built-in brain predilection—pattern-matching.

A point touching on resemblances to, or key differences from, past events familiar to the prospect feels more comfortable. An example involving a circumstance a prospect is familiar with, possibly an important recent news event, holds stronger potential to be remembered by relating a product's premise to that experience.

Repetition—confusion results when presentation content is delivered in a stream of unrelated information. Enhance recall through main-idea repetition during the presentation.

Hermann Ebbinghaus, a late 1800s researcher, determined that memories have different lifespans for different reasons. Some memories evaporate after only a few minutes; others last a lifetime. His studies demonstrated that a memory's lifespan is extended by repeating the information in intervals. The more repetitions, the higher the probability the experience will become a permanent memory.

Without repetition, whatever the experience's initial excitement may have been, retention holds high probability to be transient. ***Limit sale-call duration***—time to engage a prospect is limited—the *golden three minutes.* And, once engaged, the period to hold their attention remains finite. Cognitive research maintains that attention expires at some point between 10 and 15 minutes into a presentation.

CHAPTER NINE

Dealing with Rejection

Among selling's most salient aphorisms, *the sale begins with the first no* is paradoxical. One of selling's most potent potential handicaps is fear of the word *no*. But it's only how a salesman responds to *no* that his status is earned.

No emotionally balanced person intentionally seeks rejection. But rejection avoidance resulting from a prospect's objection is a serious handicap. Cowardice in the Game, as in most activities requiring grit to perform, eliminates the ability to participate.

Selling is unique as a profession; adversity is the norm. You learn to expect objections appearing as rejection; you don't learn to accept rejection. Appearance of rejection when objections are raised is a Game constant. There is good reason. Without controversy, and skill required to overcome buyer objections, there would be no need for a selling profession.

Objections assume:

Actual rejection; or

Interest is being shown.

One is rejection resulting from a condition; the other, a request for response to a concern.

A condition makes a sale impossible, outside your control. But an objection by a qualified prospect—room in the budget, need for your product, and authority to act—is more probably a request for clarification. Experienced salesmen understand that objections lead to a conclusion.

How objections are viewed profoundly affect sale-call outcomes: *The potential for rejection is to be aggressively avoided;* or *A feeling of detachment;* the sale process is just continuing.

Rejection avoidance triggered by an objection is emotional, never rational. Feelings, having taken control, result in a destructive reaction. You run from it, or indulge in a temperamental outburst. Either reaction hands the circumstances the trophy.

But when an objection isn't personalized, the response can be creative. What may have appeared to be a losing hand transitions to "I'll be back."

Prospects having no interest in a proposal attempt to end the interview as quickly as possible. A frequent brush-off is expressed by enthusiasm, paying heavy compliments to the salesman and his product, but delaying a decision based on any number of concerns: *I have to think about it … let me talk it over with my partner… I will have to run it by my accountant…*

When a customer puts you off he is more likely saying one of two things: he is either incapable of saying *no* for fear of how you will react if he told the truth; or his unconscious mind hasn't been provided sufficient proof to make a positive decision.

The difference between a brush-off, and an objection is that the brush-off, a rejection in disguise, implies hope. It feels good.

Objections, expressed as a challenge (I'm concerned about your pricing") have a more ominous tinge, but are necessary, even critical, to the process.

If objections aren't being encountered, seek them. Why is the product you think fits the prospect's need so well not stimulating their interest?

Anticipated objection responses are simple, to the point, rehearsed until appearing spontaneous when circumstantial need arises.

Preparing for Objections

An objection, appearing as rejection, will:

Make you quit, or make you stronger—when you bend, then respond to an objection with a creatively expressed answer, you have cleared one of The Game's first hurdles;

Give you confidence—selling is a high-risk enterprise; objections and rejection will be experienced regularly;

Rob you of your will—if a reaction to rejection is to go home or for a drive, rejection won. The alternative is to take a deep breath, stride into the middle of the situation, and show everyone; or

Sharpen your skills—a circumstance overcome makes you better. You find a way to dominate circumstances that previously would have ended your sales call.

It isn't necessary for objection response to be brilliant. But in The Game—like a professional quarterback's sense—good wiring pays off. When prepared responses are created prior to the main event, any objection can be countered.

Without anticipated objection responses, a few hidden fists out there hold potential to knock you flat. One of the more formidable—when under duress, your nonverbal language conflicts with your words. You may feel self-assured about your product knowledge, but lack of a prepared response to an objection, such as the price issue, holds high potential for losing control of the call.

When an objection is actually rejection, coping with feelings and behaviors calls for an honest assessment of your typical reaction when past rejection-troll visitation was experienced:

How did I feel? Fearful? Angry? What about ... neither. It isn't sensible to feel emotional about someone not needing your product right now, or even getting in your face about their disinterest. There will be another day. And, when there is, you will be there.

What form of rejection was experienced? A polite, *no thank you?* A disinterested, *I don't think so?* A furious, *get the #!*@x out of here and don't come back?* The gist attached to all is "We won't be doing business today, will we?"

How did I respond? Several options are available, but everyone when rejected will resort to a particular habitual reaction:

Passive: Stuttering, dry mouth, sweaty palms, an imitation of an abused cur slinking out, tail between the legs. Possibly muttering a weak apology for having interrupted their day.

Aggressive: "Same to you, Jack," "Nobody talks to me like that ..." or suggestions for a few unattractive actions to be taken.

Creative: "I've caught you at a bad time. I'll get back to you when it's more convenient to your schedule."

Of course, door number three. No need to react; you will be back.

Inadequate responses make a clear statement—preparation for the discussion was not given sufficient importance. Now the circumstances exact the full measure of consequence.

A prepared sales call is confident. If circumstances turn dark, composure remains unflappable. You are 007. Bond, James Bond. Responding calmly, an objection is answered with a word picture: "Your options are to stay with what you are doing and plan to take longer to do the job, or get a bigger hammer."

For developing capable responses to anticipated objections, a valuable tool is a script book. With experience, the most effective responses with certain social styles will evolve.

What to Do, and Not Do, With Rejection

Dealing with a negative circumstance will challenge you. The response can be positive, or can send you further down the emotional scale:

A positive view may imagine that results were better than what actually happened;

A negative view imagines outcomes were worse than reality.

The first few days of selling experience hold high probability of appearing as a series of panic attacks. When confronted with skepticism answering objections will likely be very different than how you feel, or habitually respond when confronted by hostile-appearing circumstances.

Depersonalizing objections appearing as rejection is among personal brand development's first objectives. The depersonalization process begins with an understanding—no matter how seemingly personalized or intense an objection may appear, it cannot be personal when it comes from someone who doesn't know you.

It may be that the first impression you made didn't work this time. Or the other person's hostility just selected you as the moment's convenient dog to kick. Under either, the belt is tightened, you get on with your day. You have:

Prepared yourself—a golfer experiences a bad round occasionally; the fisherman has days when the fish don't bite; The Game has days when it seems nothing goes right—even when lack of preparation wasn't the reason.

Avoided personalizing rejection—when actual rejection is experienced it's your proposition, not you, being rejected. When you leave an encounter that hasn't gone particularly well, pull your thoughts together, and move on to another prospect.

Dealt with rejection like any other exercise—acceptance of rejection is at first difficult. You get bruised and sore. But the more you deal with rejection, the stronger you become. Eventually, when Game conditions are at their bleakest, you're at your best.

Avoided misdirection—the urge to avoid rejection may result in the desire to change a presentation's format. But a watered-down presentation in hopes the customer will not say *no* is a losing proposition. Make the presentation stronger.

Before rejection fear has been recognized for the destructively irrational reaction it is, and has been relegated to its proper place, you fake it. You say to yourself "I needed that *no* to get on with my next call." Trite? Yes. It also works. And has worked for anyone who has made The Game their profession.

The Mere Exposure Effect

Setting aside rejection fear's emotional attachments, the *Mere Exposure Effect*, also known as the *Familiarity Effect*, soundly supports the salesman's legendary persistence.

Proof of what any experienced Game participant comes to know through experience, the Mere Exposure Effect was identified in the late 19th century by Gustav Fechner who discovered that people tend to develop preferences for individuals or things more familiar to them. Contemporary Mere Exposure Effect research continued with Robert Zajonc, a leading expert in human behavior.

Dr. Zajonc, dedicating much of his career to study of the link between repetition of any arbitrary stimulus, and the affection people develop for it, concluded that the effect of repetition on liking is a profoundly important biological act, extending to all animals. Repeated exposure increases familiarity, and people develop a preference for individuals more familiar to them.

What is known is the more often a person is exposed to someone, the more probable they will be seen as likeable. And with likeability comes confidence in ability and trustworthiness.

The Mere Exposure Effect is of particular value when dealing with sufficiently self-satisfied types who will claim "there never has been, or ever will be, a need for your product." You of course will acknowledge their position, then prepare for the next contact with them.

Eventually the light will come on and you will have your moment. These prospects just need some time, possibly proof, to see the value of what you have to offer. If added effort is needed to arrive at a positive conclusion, no problem. That, after all, is The Game's mission.

Once beyond acquiring The Game's basic elements, a natural progression is to develop the personal brand—acknowledged selling competence—of a GameBreaker.

PART THREE

PERSONAL BRAND DEVELOPMENT

CHAPTER TEN

Creating Your Personal Brand

Personal Development's Role

Part One addressed what The Game is about, and described a few characteristics essential to successful Game participation. Part Two described Game participants, and how best to approach them.

Now we turn to how a selling neophyte can develop the *personal product*, the behaviors and habits consistent with succeeding at The Game, be acquired in the most efficient manner possible.

Like any other profession, Game participants experience their productive days and their rough periods. Early in a sales career there may be times when challenges extend beyond acquiring the necessary selling skills, to working mainly to make ends meet.

But, in the best scenario, you discover that you love the work. Something about it makes you want to come back day after day; to be better in September than you were in March.

Succeeding at selling assumes the presence of certain needed attributes. As applies to several skilled professions, selling is a craft, requiring development of a particular set of skills dedicated to the activity. You become a doctor by studying medicine or a lawyer by studying law. It's no less challenging to become a dominant salesman than to become a capable surgeon.

As in those professions, or a competitive sport, selling skills are learned through study and application. Some skills may have been inherited; others will be developed.

Competitive achievement begins as a dream. Even Tom Brady picked up a football for the first time. Some seem to have a genetic predisposition for certain things to come easier than for others, but most have to work at it; work hard until an epiphany—mind, body, and spirit in sync—says "I can do this." Such moments change your life.

Everyone is born with, or acquires very early, certain talents. This might lead to a conclusion that, because needed skills weren't inherited, you can't do some things you may want to do. But, not so. Considerable research has disclosed people succeed more because of *what* they do, rather than who they are.

Personal branding, how the personal product you will develop to compete in The Game is approached, begins with: what would you like to be? How would you like to be perceived? What do you need to know? Where are you short in required skills?

Developing a Personal Brand

An aspiring salesman has little more on which to base his assumptions about what constitutes a salesman's life than does a small boy who, having seen a fireman at work, decides a fireman is what he wants to be. Developing the means to participate begins with an assessment: what do you bring to the event? And what skills can be added? A few attributes evident in successful salespeople may already be in your possession:

Some degree of selling knowledge;

A few applicable personal strengths;

Some latent personal capabilities to build on; and

A dedicated desire to succeed at the activity.

Some going-in potential advantages may be tempered by other less productive habits and behaviors. This group represents opportunity. Positive behaviors require no attention; you have those working for you now.

Until competence required to perform effectively is acquired, career beginnings from one initiate to another may illustrate marked similarities. Personal-development needs will differ, but assume acquiring:

Expert knowledge of the product to be sold, and its competitive environment; and

Skills required to creatively represent the product's best needs-satisfying qualities.

The learning process combines:

Maintenance learning—passive. Adjusting as-needed to conditions as they *appear to be;* or

Innovative learning—active. Adapting to conditions *as they are;* changing a few behaviors needed to make things happen, as you decide them to happen.

Initial activity favors accelerated innovative learning—absorbing product knowledge as quickly as possible. In the process, you identify the behaviors required of a capable salesman, supplemented by seminars, articles, books, and mentoring from experienced individuals willing to give some of their time and knowledge.

But there is a caveat—your *perception* of facts encountered during the learning process. Viewpoints—opinions, prejudices, personal values—affect perceptions of conditions as they appear, not necessarily as they actually are.

The learning process remains constant, imposing lifelong need for adapting to evolving circumstances as the sales role extends from entry-level, to the expertise needed to satisfy an increasingly more demanding clientele.

The Path of Least Resistance

Selling, like most challenging occupations, has a *fundamental unity*—a sense of how the activity goes together. The Game's fundamental unity combines product-knowledge superiority with personal effectiveness.

It's possible to become moderately successful with uncommonly well-informed product knowledge, or through acquiring unusually capable selling skills. But extraordinary Game success results only from superiority in both.

Unlike more literal professional knowledge development, the path to personal-effectiveness superiority is not so readily apparent. Facts memorization requires little imagination; personal effectiveness is unique to the individual, depending on behaviors under stress and development of prepared responses to challenges.

How circumstances are viewed, how stress impacts ability to perform, and habits influencing how the individual goes about their day all influence personal effectiveness.

Metaphorically, professional knowledge and personal effectiveness are two independent streams, combining to make a river. Each stream forms independently, neither holding initial dominance, each dependent on the other to achieve a significant river.

The professional knowledge stream is composed of the product-to-be-sold's need-satisfying qualities, the competitive environment, an understanding of customer needs, and ability to speak the market's specialized language. *Market sense,* the epiphany when you *get it,* is still to come.

Achieving competence in the shortest period possible is a worthy objective, but one without shortcuts. The process is evolutionary, progressive steps taking you from point "A" to point "B," then from "B" to "C"… It isn't possible to move directly to "Z" from "A."

If a few needed Game behaviors have not been part of your personal make-up, Game behaviors are eminently capable of being cultivated, just as they have been by every individual who dominates among The Game's best players.

One particular Game-changing capability to cultivate is a creative competence required to persuasively frame the product's need-satisfying qualities. Framing transforms relevant facts into a word picture, a story.

An element of theater illuminates a main idea's premise. Describing a tranquil park-like setting can't be done by listing facts such as the varieties and numbers of landscape elements, or an included pond's size, content, and depth. A picture requires a story:

"A scene of tranquility consistent with the world's great gardens. A mirrored lake set off by flowering trees and shrubbery artistically dispersed over manicured rolling lawns. A sanctuary for wildlife, and individuals attracted to an atmosphere of quiet contemplation."

The salesman's potential genius is in the framing. And, like the skill required for driving a racecar or playing a sport professionally, personal-effectiveness improvement has no end point. The train pulling into a station is a point on the trip; down the tracks another station waits.

CHAPTER ELEVEN

The Personal-Development Process

Personal effectiveness progress is possible because personal effective-ness learning is cumulative.

And at personal effectiveness's heart is a system, an organized approach to how the work can best be done.

Game-behavior development is most effective when given top-of-mind attention. And a decision to make a behavioral change, once made, can rely on the *Rule of Consistency* to take over. What initially required thought will come as naturally as the tacit knowledge you know already—driving a car, walking, or speaking.

Tacit Learning

Like a concert pianist's skill, a professional quarterback's passing prowess, riding a bicycle, or driving a car, selling skill is tacit.

A learned, subjectively defined, process tacit skill is objectively understood, but not capable of being accurately described. And like other skills requiring expertise, it's not unusual for Game aspirants to begin their career floundering. The high beams initially just not reaching far enough.

Learning to drive by reading a *rules-of-the-road* manual is no more practical than training to be a chef through reading a cookbook, or learning to ride a bicycle by having the process explained. Explanations are useful, but experience is necessary to achieve something that initially may seem overwhelming.

In Polanyi Mihaly's philosophical *Theory of Knowledge* he observed "We learn to swim or dance without being able to explain precisely how it was done. We recognize a friend's face without being able to specify exactly what we recognize ... The speed and complexity of this integration easily outstrips the relatively ponderous processes of logic, or inference."

For certain skills, such as apply to The Game, knowledge acquired through study can be of use, but requires becoming tacit: "Once we have learned to drive a car, the manual is set aside, and left to the tacit operations of the developed skill."

Selling, in similar manner, is more art than science. It requires order, but also feeds on a certain randomness, and constantly challenges. As a result, as with most successful endeavors requiring skill, selling skill develops in stages. All at once would be an attractive thought, but not an option.

If there were only a few characteristics needed many people would be able to pull it off just by following a recipe. But the chemistry involved makes the apparently explainable, unexplainable.

You may not understand how you arrived at a point where you *get it*, when your mind bypasses logical deliberation, but experience has taken you there.

Driving at first required conscious awareness of every movement: parking the car, merging into traffic, changing lanes, backing into the neighbor's yard ... But with practice the activity became routine. Game participation is like that.

The subjective question "How much do I need to know to succeed at The Game?" leads to an equally subjective answer: depends on *succeeding*'s definition.

If succeeding means a casual, *enough-to-make-a-living* mind-set, learning will more probably evolve from day-to-day experience; on-the-job-training as the primary source of knowledge. Whatever can be absorbed through osmosis is *enough,* a self-determined path of least-resistance.

But personal development relying only on random experience is not an easy road, a two-laner with a lot of diesel trucks and trailers driven by some really bad attitudes.

The Game's road has its rules, and rules ignored can be negative in consequence for the glad-to-just-be-there group making up the 80% of salesmen who collectively generate 20% of the selling universe's income.

The alternate group—the 20% who achieve *best-in-the-business* status—never tops out at what they are aware they *need* to know. For them, innovative learning will tap every available resource, and search for more.

For all, the personal-development process is evolutionary, extending from infancy, through childhood and adolescence, into maturity. Latent potential allows just about anyone willing to develop the capabilities required to succeed to do so. The uncertain ingredient is not just "What do you want?" but "What you are willing to do to get it?"

The Individual Who Will Participate

Accomplished salesmen represent a particular kind of success; their careers, long arcs of intense dedication.

Skilled activities rely on two components, the:

Practical tools required to fulfill the activity; and

Personal qualities needed to put the tools to work.

Initially the personal branding you develop will be like a machine with some important parts missing. In this instance, behaviors. The learning process accommodates the condition with attention given to developing the needed parts.

There is no question when some are born the fairies seem to have been kinder, providing them with certain advantages—imagination, industry, eloquence, intelligence. But there are also certain essential denials that have the apparent effect of balancing the scales—judgment, will to succeed, character, work ethic …

The occasional individual may be gifted with some of The Game's more outwardly apparent essential characteristics, but not to be confused with the phenomenon referred to as a *born salesman*, a 19th century social invention long past its useful life.

Salespeople are not born any more than a doctor or lawyer is born. They are made, then continually polished through a career-long growth process; more doors opening as skills advance.

The combination of qualities you bring to the event is among the circumstances' most consistent variables. Three alternative versions of you will participate:

The person you think you are: how you see yourself. This is the *you* referred to as your *self*, largely a reflection of your sense of self-esteem. Low self-esteem and you will think you are either more, or less, than you are; high self-esteem, and you will be satisfied you are up to the task. The high self-esteem's attitude? Bring it!

The person your prospect thinks you are: sale prospects will form an opinion of you and your intent based on their view of salespeople in the first place, and their first impression of you. You have no control over the former; the latter, barring an unfortunate resemblance to one of your prospect's less likeable relatives, is mostly yours to determine.

The person you actually are: an entity psychologists refer to as the *Authentic Self,* a highly individualized bundle of attitudes, habits, and behaviors, some possibly a little quirky. The real, and the only, you.

The other two yous are fabrications, formed by you and others with whom you interact. A few legacy behaviors accrued from your formative years will play a role in how the actual you is capable of performing. Most important, your behavior when placed under pressure, or challenged: an emotion-fueled reaction; or a mature, free-of-emotion, response.

Some years ago, the psychologist Timothy Wilson wrote about this particular you in "Strangers to Ourselves." You have now been introduced to the hidden you in control of much of what the more outwardly apparent you does, although you may have rarely had an objective glimpse of him.

Personal brand development begins with assessing how these representative yous will interact as you develop selling behaviors.

We prefer to think of ourselves as *ourselves;* that doesn't change. As you develop selling behaviors, becoming a salesman isn't an identity; it's simply a part of your actual self, as you develop Game competence.

Know thyself, an aphorism attributed to the Greek philosophers, was clarified in the Suda, a 10th-century encyclopedia of Greek knowledge. The meaning of know thyself was defined to be "Applied to those whose boasts exceed what they are." With that understanding, needed behaviors are more easily determined.

Personal effectiveness presumes acquiring an essential understanding of certain human tendencies.

It isn't necessary to become a psychologist to make productive use of a few principles pulled from the psychology playbook. The ability to recognize certain tendencies—yours, and your prospect's—is a dominant Game advantage to be acquired, an attribute beginning with a personal assessment of characteristics you bring to the event:

Your habits and behaviors: As you are now, as you can become if you choose, what The Game requires to become a high-order competitor; and

Your prospect's potential behaviors and motivations: As they are, rather than as you previously may have assumed them to be, or should be, and the most-productive approaches available to complete a sale.

Habitual behaviors, guiding the person you actually are, are default settings. Other than when the occasion calls for another setting, habits applied to a particular activity eliminate the need to think when a response best suited for the occasion is appropriate.

The psychology profession maintains that we are not entirely responsible for the way we are, but we most definitely are responsible for what we become. Toward that end it may be necessary to let go of a possibly cherished idea or two of your *self* as you perceive him to be.

In The Game you will deal with your prospects' versions of the same three individuals. The considerable advantage you hold is that your Authentic Self is capable of consciously influencing how the *you* your prospect thinks you are comes across.

To acquire a better understanding of the real you occasional introspection is sensible. For the most part we are not very good at understanding our own subjectivity, but unless there is a bullet-proof aversion to soul searching, prepared responses to a few frequently-raised questions can be of use:

What do you care most about in your business life? Truly care?

If you were to write your own obituary, how would you want it to read as it relates to your career?

What is your physical appearance? How do you feel about it? Does it affect you?

What do you fear most? Irrational fears, not the truly scary kind.

What are your major strengths of character—integrity. work ethic, dependability, truthfulness ...? Possible flaws?

What are some of your: unproductive habits? Annoying habits? Really good habits?

What are you good at? What are you not good at, but wish you were?

If you could do just one thing, and know you would be successful, what would it be?

What are some childhood events that helped shape you into the person you are today?

"Behind it all" describes areas of behavioral improvement to pursue if you aren't yet where you need to be. It's philosophical, but supported by plenty of historical fact.

What if you were to wake up tomorrow morning, the slate scrubbed clean? What would be the first skills you would want to recover to continue on as a Game participant? Would learning to understand the spoken word, and writing capabilities, be top priorities? What about an understanding of motivations—your own, and others? These are basic Game skills required under any circumstance.

An inherent tension between the desire to *be your own person,* and meaningful involvement in The Game, is a test of resolve. A natural preference is to think of ourselves as being just *who I am*, and leave it at that.

The process of becoming a salesman doesn't preempt the view, but making only one change in how something may have been done habitually can turn an entire Game approach around. It comes down to making a few choices.

The Consequence of Choice

The universe is populated by those who desire success, but on their terms. They want it their way. *Why should I have to do all that? Why can't I just continue as I am?*

But change for anyone aspiring to master selling as a profession, as opposed to a job, is critical to the personal development process. It is necessary to adapt to The Game's needs.

Change is not a layup; people love familiarity and patterns. They cling to them. The phenomenon is so entrenched that it can only be chalked up to your nature. But attributing a behavior to human nature doesn't mean you have to be controlled by it.

Just about every Western-tradition philosopher since Plato has placed a premium on the autonomy of choice, each choice displaying individual character through asserting a sometimes rampant need for self-expression.

In "A Logic of Expressive Choice" Alexander A. Schuessler observed, "Some choices have only a *this is who I am* function: foods we eat; cars we drive; the house we live in; preferred music; books read; hobbies pursued; political viewpoints … are expressive choices." No connection to practical importance, expressive choices aren't made to produce an outcome.

Expressive choices tell the world what an individual cares about. In more readily apparent form manner of dress, a clear statement of taste, sends a message: "I am serious," "I am sensible," "I am rich," or, "I wear what I want, and I don't care how anyone feels about it." Substantive choices are made with intent to cause something to happen.

You aren't alone if you haven't determined exactly where your intensity meter has to be set to become effective. But substantive choices will be made when conscious improvement of your effectiveness is the objective.

Selling is a problem-solving business. You will be responsible in some way for activity outcomes. The condition imposes need for certain behaviors required of Game participation.

Substantive choices can be as simple as making a few incremental improvements in how to conduct yourself under challenging circumstances. But the possible presence of a serious tripwire to change can result from presence of a built-in *governor,* the ego—the *inner voice* described in philosophical writings—constantly acting to disrupt the best of intentions.

Rational thinking never enters into this voice's considerations. It doesn't take into account that competence developed may not yet be satisfactory to proceed to the level the more rational voice knows is required.

"Why do we need to change?" "We've done okay so far, haven't we?" "Why take the risk?" "Let's just keep doing what we're doing— things will work out." "If people don't like me as I am, that's just too bad." "Sure we want to get the job done, but there has to be a little fun along the way."

Among the most effective hindrances to an all-out, let's-get-it-on attack mode toward personal development effectiveness is anyone's natural resistance to change. If that description doesn't fit you, congratulations. But if it does, it only means that now you know, and can now do something about it.

Choices as profound as Albert Camus' "Should I kill myself, or have a cup of coffee?" are unusual. But to his point, life is about constant choices, some more extreme than others. In every moment of every day choices are weighed among alternatives, most made without conscious thought.

At some point in the process you decide you are a salesman, and begin to act like one. A few revelations will be based on intense thinking, but most of what will be experienced will result from pragmatic choices, on-the-run-adaptations made to rapidly shifting circumstances.

When a choice is made to transform a shortcoming into a productive behavior, need for conscious decision is eliminated. The fledgling becomes a bird of prey:

Gaining control over negative behaviors;

Acquiring real selling skills—a personal brand of your own making;

Changing some unproductive habits you have been comfortable with until now; and

Developing the ability to memorably communicate relevant thoughts, to motivate others.

But change, even when positive, isn't sudden. Positive change is slow and steady, a result of consistent attention to the process.

Your Personal Plan—Writing Your Story's Narrative

Developing a personal brand is better understood when depicted in a story. Selling competence results from a quest, one in which the seeker transforms. A personal story—evolving by conscious intent, or unconsciously—that you will write for yourself.

So the story begins—*once upon a time*—because as we know, every good story begins that way. And since you are the author, you can choose to make it a good story. You as the questor set out to accomplish something, in the process overcoming conflict; the basic structure of any good story.

The Game dictates encountering some circumstances no one would likely want to face. But learning how to deal with the circumstances is what keeps The Game so interesting. Serious conflict is expected, and necessary:

First, what the main character wants must be challenging: risking something to achieve something. The more difficult, the better; more risk makes the story more interesting. Sure you joined the Navy, but did you volunteer to become a Navy Seal? Achieve Seal status? There needs to be uncertainty—will the character make it? Will he defeat, or be defeated by, the dragon; and

The quest must require sacrifice: some pain experienced. Picture yourself succeeding. Making use of imagery paint an end-result picture: what it looks like; the skills required to achieve it; what you are going to do; and how you will do it. The story's prequel is a description of what has happened to you until now, by happenstance.

In "Travels with Charlie," John Steinbeck placed his version of a story in perspective:

"Once a journey is designed, equipped, put in process, a new factor enters and takes over. A trip, a safari, an exploration, is an entity, different from all other journeys. It has personality, temperament, individuality, uniqueness. A journey is a person in itself, no two are alike. We find after years of struggle that we do not take a trip, it takes us … In this a journey is like a marriage. The certain way to be wrong is to think you control it."

It isn't necessarily comfortable to be the main character. Remarkable stories require heroic characters to act affirmatively, facing conflict with courage. An unremarkable story requires none of that.

The process of becoming a salesman is a condensed version of life. The role evolving from beginner, with all the beginner's shortcomings, to mastery of a business profession coming closest to a true professional sport.

The novice transforms—from a bundle of prior behaviors, some of use, others not—through acquisition of a few new behaviors specific to The Game's requirements.

Only selling doesn't afford time to *find* yourself before things get serious. The burdens of the hunt begin overnight, forcing an immediate reach for previously undisclosed inner resources.

Psychologists observe that an experience of this sort "causes a regressive disorganization of the personality that, when skillfully handled, can lead to a constructive reorganization of the individual's capabilities." The questor having faced the dragons, and survived the encounter, is now better prepared to risk it all again.

You will get a taste for a story of your choice when your personal-development process has been organized into some form of structure. Then, having lived a more productive story, an actual character of your own making will emerge, having learned a few things through experience.

The story will evolve into a sleeper, or a real page-turner, depending on how the engine to power this train is assembled:

The personal brand you expect to bring to the event;

The strategies and personal objectives, as you see them, required to make your story achievable;

The process you will follow in developing your personal product;

Steps the narrative is to take;

How progress is to be measured;

Where you are in the development process, as the process evolves; and

How much further you have to go before the story develops into what you planned.

This story deals only with the future, and how actions taken will affect that future. With the objectives kept reasonable, simply *being good* gives way to *getting better.* Setbacks from ineffective behavior are recognized; a more suitable-to-the-occasion action, substituted.

How selling competence develops depends on the story's quality. There is good reason for pursuing extreme competence as the story's outcome.

CHAPTER TWELVE

Developing a Learning Strategy

Managing Personal Competence Development

Other things equal, extreme selling competence leaves competitors in the dust.

Knowledge superiority can provide a competitive edge, but notably capable selling skills will catapult you over the competition—even if the competition knows more, and has been in the business longer.

Personal growth associated with developing Game skills isn't about reinventing the personal *you*—the *self* you know and may very well prefer. It *is* about developing some selling-related behaviors to be applied when circumstances challenge. The bricks and mortar—habitual behaviors:

Acquired by happenstance, through prior experience; or

Cultivated, as planned by intent, through focused training.

Every academic learning study has illustrated equivalent results: focused attention improves retention, accuracy, and clarity in just about any subject—writing, math, science … In college it was hours of study.

The process hasn't changed. What you learn can be a result of targeted training, or simply the product of experience. One, deliberate; the other, by chance.

A salesman's characteristics, like those required of a quarterback, are a mixture of courage, toughness, instincts, preparation, resourcefulness, and a few other less tangible variables.

Game participation relies on cultivated behaviors applied specifically to the salesman's role—activities essential to developing formidable personal effectiveness:

Creating a dynamic personal story—a written narrative: objectives, and how you will achieve them;

Managing your time—conscious application of time usage;

Understanding Game fundamentals—Game skills development is equivalent to learning any sport. For baseball, the basics—hitting, throwing, and catching the ball.

With selling: acquiring an understanding of human psychology, constructing a formalized sale-process format, developing habits and behaviors needed to execute the sale process, and how to close a sale;

Adopting a dominant image—you will be perceived in some manner. Through conscious intent, or through habits controlling your behaviors, you project an image. The better is, by intent, how you will present yourself. The acquired image formed around a role incorporating some new behaviors;

Becoming an authority on your product and its market—you are surrounded by resources: read voraciously, research the Internet, get to know knowledgeable people on the subject …;

An extreme ability to engage—selling is about the other person: their needs, their reaction to you, what you have to say, and how you say it. You can be an interesting conversationalist by simply asking questions. Not probing inquiries, just an effort to draw the other person out.

To some, this particular skill seems to come more easily. If you are not among the gifted, practice it. Until a new habit is formed;

Accepting mistakes' value—The Game's strategies are perfected through trial and error. Mistakes are vital to knowledge developed through experience;

Seeing yourself as already successful—individuals who succeed are equipped with an *I-can-do-this* mindset. The attitude implies substance, even when competence is still-to-come;

Identifying the most pressing current personal need to address—the answer may identify a half-dozen self-improvement opportunities; focus on one. Get the first one where it needs to be, then attack the rest, one at a time;

Understanding pursuit of unreasonable goals, or rushing the process, will more probably result in reduced effectiveness—a natural desire will be to hit it into the light tower, but competence developed through experience comes first. Determine to be better in September than you were in March;

Resisting collapse into self-doubt when competence isn't progressing as you feel it should—big aspirations are useful, but need tempering. You will hear about others' successes. Ignore them. They only prove what can be done.

Avoid comparing your status with someone else's, or some imagined idea of how things *ought to be*. Persistent individuals have time on their side; the impatient are more inclined to lose their nerve.

To be human is to be born with a drive to accomplish. Aristotle described a *life-growth-achievement principle* as inherent to every human being. He observed "Human beings have a natural desire and capacity to know, and should use their abilities to their fullest potential through exercise of their realized capacities." When an individual achieves something worthwhile the success gratifies, creating a sense of worth.

The personal-development process is a quest, one that starts with beginner's luck, then proceeds to punish the participant relentlessly until one of two conditions emerge: a considerably evolved individual who has become stronger for the experience; or an individual who gave in to weakness, and quit.

Fortunately, unlike professional athletics or quantum physics, succeeding at The Game doesn't require having been an accident of nature. What you don't know you can learn if you have an understanding of how to learn, and a willingness to act. Selling, like succeeding at anything, is a consequence of mastering the subject's nuances.

Emphasis is placed on acquiring behaviors critical to Game effectiveness.

CHAPTER THIRTEEN

Behavior's Role in The Game

The means to participate in The Game is developed.

The first condition is to determine what behaviors you bring to The Game; then determine what needs to be added. Some legacy behaviors may be useful to Game participation; others will require attention. Certain legacy behaviors possibly holding influence over your life says nothing at all of their validity.

Habitual Behaviors

Behaviors reside in habits. Certain behaviors are of extreme value; others are essential.

Old habits are comfortable, and, even when limiting, are addictive. Like any addiction, habitual behaviors can be immensely controlling. The better you understand why you do some of what you do, the more effective you will be at making needed adjustments to Game participation.

Actions requiring flashes of insight—such as when an objection is raised—are subject to different rules than well-considered thought. When immediate action is required, reflecting on how to best deal with a need at hand is a process-destroyer. It's the same paralysis-through-analysis found in sports contexts. Lose the flow; lose The Game.

As with any competitive sport, certain behaviors peculiar to the event are developed. High-stakes selling situations don't allow for well-thought-out purely rational decision-making. The circumstances having stated their position, it's your move. Carefully considered options are out; the unconscious mind makes a decision, and takes action. But there is a qualifier.

What if the old habits, instead of acting assertively, self-destruct when circumstances trigger an aggressive reaction—negative behaviors asserting themselves. Spur of the moment action is considerably susceptible to how habitual behaviors are capable of responding.

Habits guide mindless, no-thought-needed, behavior—behavior that's just a part of *what you do*. Formed from past experience, habits, when you are placed under pressure, determine how you will likely react to certain circumstances.

The problem is that legacy behaviors—developed at another time, under different conditions—are such a part of what we do that they will fight to prevent intrusive new behaviors required of Game participation from interfering with the *self* you know.

But hanging on tightly to old behaviors makes it difficult to accept new ones. The condition requires recognition—it's irrational. You meet the need for change head-on, or through the more effective approach to implementing behavioral changes—through small grassroots improvements. However you do it, you do it.

Robert Pirsig in, "Zen and The Art of Motorcycle Maintenance," saw the problem as:

"What you have to do if you get caught in this gumption trap of value rigidity is slow down. You are going to have to slow down anyway, whether you want to or not. But slow down deliberately, and go over ground that you've been over before to see if things you thought were important were really important. Watch it the way you watch a line when fishing, and before long as sure as you live, you will get a little nibble, a little fact asking in a timid, humble way if you are interested in it. That's the way the world keeps on happening; be interested in it.

After a while you may find that the nibbles you get are more interesting than your original purpose of maintaining a sense of self. When that happens you've reached a kind of point of arrival. Then you are no longer strictly a technician—you are becoming the artist. You've conquered the gumption trap of value rigidity."

You would be unusual if you weren't put off by change in the legacy habits and behaviors you know as comfortable. Change attaches uncertainty; uncertainty produces stress.

And that brings out one of old habit's most dedicated advocates—the ego.

The Ego's Role in Habitual Behaviors

The keeper of the keys to the habitual-behavior cache is a formidable, potentially highly disruptive, force—the human ego. The ego aggressively guards the self-described *limits of reason* applied to habitual behaviors, resisting the very idea of change.

Based entirely on emotion, negative behaviors in the best of science fiction are capable of rising up, taking over, and living through their host as though they were the only you.

A few of the ego's more destructive behaviors, and how to deal with them, are apparent:

Limited ability to perform under stress—a tendency to react in fear or anger to an uncomfortable circumstance is replaced by thoughtful response, dealing assertively when adversity calls for a steady hand.

A tendency to procrastinate—waiting to complete important activities until the last minute is replaced by *do-it-now!*

A casual approach to personal appearance—a first impression is made once. Making the first impression positive reinforces your role. An easily controlled example is dress. A business-like appearance communicates that you are collected and ready to work.

Poor time usage—time is a currency, spent as you choose, or by default. *Time well-spent* is a hallmark attributable to The Game's most notable participants.

If you see yourself in any of these, know them as opportunities. It isn't probable that you will act in a manner contrary to your habitual behaviors, unless the satisfaction of having resisted the insufficient habit outweighs the stress of having resisted it.

Old negative behaviors are addictive, and survive only because the carrier is unable to deal with them. Addicts to any destructive behavior can articulate their behavior's consequences, then proceed to fail in acting in their own best interests.

Fortunately, habits can be modified. When you begin to live a new behavior as though you own it you will have arrived at the next level. Tomorrow you get the better of the new behavior partially, then do it again one day at a time. In a few weeks a more sufficient habit will have replaced the offending behavior.

And among negative behaviors is one of The Game's most virulent nemeses: fear, the irrational kind.

Irrational Fears

Fear can be real, based on danger, and perfectly rational; or it can be psychological, near entirely irrational.

Rational fear reflects common sense. You don't play in freeway traffic, or jump off high places. But irrational fear can be a real troublemaker.

Carryovers from the past, irrational fears are not objective. But like a hard-to-get-rid-of, spare-bedroom-occupying relative, they are interruptive, and can be harder to evict than the unwanted roomer.

Irrational fears fuel a variety of hang-ups, ranging from quirky, *step on a crack, break your mother's back*, to some really disturbed phobias. Some of the choicest include fear of:

Rejection—being told *no* in any form;

Failure—inability to admit to a mistake, or the expectation you might not be able to do something expected of you;

Being "found out"—the possibility that you aren't as good as others have assumed you are; you aren't as knowledgeable as you are *supposed to be*.

Every beginning salesman must learn to deal with such fears. Courage, useful in the common affairs of life, is essential to selling. Even casual familiarity with any of these unwarranted hang-ups requires assertive action to overcome.

Stressful encounters result in a reaction, or a response. Reaction—with fear or anger—will result in backing away from, or an aggressive retort to, a perceived condition. In contrast, a response is composed—an assertive, emotion-free addressing of at-the-moment needs.

You can't necessarily make these fears go away. You just have to have something bigger than the fear to go after. Successful salesmen don't eliminate fear, they just overcome it.

Personal Characteristics Absolutely Needed

A commonly held viewpoint attributes selling success to a special affinity with people that results in making an individual naturally likeable.

But, if valid, the definition applies only at a selling career's earliest stages. This popular view of the born-sales type has been considerably diminished in contemporary professional selling, a result of customers having become more sophisticated, more skeptical, and requiring focus be placed on their needs.

A take-over-the-room personality can be a powerful asset when combined with substance. But, taken alone, supremely confident demeanor is no substitute for gaining a prospect's trust and confidence through a genuine focus on their need.

Contemporary selling places emphasis on personal characteristics commonly exhibited by highly successful individuals:

A demeanor of supreme self-confidence;

Uncompromising commitment to succeeding;

Exceptional, customer-oriented, service standards;

A notable sense of integrity; and

A Midwestern farmer's work ethic.

To devotees of a disciplined approach to what they do, if there is a selling *knack* it develops from the presence of those distinctions.

Acquiring Selling Behaviors

What makes some people happy outgoing extroverts, while others are timid, withdrawn, and socially inept?

To a clinical psychologist, reasons for the latter condition would be numerous. Becoming an extrovert isn't necessary, but behavioral tendencies influenced by feelings of inadequacy are going to require a fundamental decision: what kind of horse will you ride in this race? Plow horse? Pony? Racehorse?

The choices simplify. Keep doing things as you have been doing them, and expect the same outcomes, or try a new strategy, making adjustments until a way that works for you emerges.

If you are resigned to doing one thing one way forever, without ever improving, there will be little pleasure in the process; only the same deadening routine.

The transition is familiar to anyone who has succeeded at The Game. A narrow ledge, sloping two ways, divides what the old habits are screaming to preserve, and what circumstances impose.

On the ledge's one slope old habits offer the status quo, the easy way; on the other, hard work, and the stress of meeting the circumstances head-on.

Habits are vital to routine activities. They protect us from the need to think through daily routine actions that would otherwise occupy thoughts.

A predetermined this-is-how-I-do-it-every-time behavioral response to a particular circumstance eliminates the need to sift through of-the-moment facts. When an *I've-seen-this-before* issue requiring an immediate coherent response is the need, a prepared response will be at the ready.

An opposite approach was taken by Arthur Miller's *Death of a Salesman* character, Willy Loman. Willy saw his ability to sell as based on his well-developed sense of what was needed to make people like him. But all the while Willie was experiencing a consistently notable lack of success, he tenaciously affirmed likeability as the ticket to great selling.

Contemporary selling leaves the Willy Lomans to contemplate their philosophical commitment to the cult of the Golden Retriever, turning instead to Attila the Hun's uncompromised dedication to extreme competence. Attila wasn't concerned with likeability, but he *was* fully committed to winning; better, never accepting losing.

At some point between Willy's and Attila's views lies a balance. This personalized compromise will require that some behaviors be developed by intent, others through the experience of trial and error.

Change isn't a layup. It's natural to love familiarity and patterns; to cling to them. The phenomenon is so entrenched that it can only be chalked up to human nature. But attributing a limiting behavior to human nature doesn't mean you have to be controlled by it.

Making changes in some behaviors—positive-thinking hype aside—isn't easy, but it can be done. In my own experience I did succeed in making a few needed adjustments, and I still work on others.

Change in habits initially may require some self-denial. Attention given to more of the so-called *right* foods; cutting back on the (also so-called) *wrong* foods; setting the alarm to bound out of bed early enough in the early morning to go out and sweat. It's all the same.

For me, some of these new habits weren't particularly unsettling; others took some getting used to. I didn't just suddenly buy into them. But eventually, after the usual denials of need for all that, I came to see modification of a few of them as just part of my story's narrative.

The quest to get to where I wanted to be, or at least headed in that direction, had its challenges. What I learned was that spending an hour or so a day, giving attention to the things that need to be done, holds immense value. The evolution from Game novice, to capable participant, brought considerable personal reward.

The result didn't come overnight, but progress was steady, a transition through a series of competence improvements.

CHAPTER FOURTEEN

Personal Development Progression

The Game has its hierarchy. Every participant has experienced a spectrum of Game competence progression:

Beginner

A beginning salesman's competence is in raw potential. Product knowledge and acquisition of Game behaviors are to come.

Beginning activity first addresses facts absorption, developing basic product knowledge, and introduction to basic selling techniques; the ABCs of Game understandings are memorized. The beginner doesn't yet comprehend what is being absorbed.

This part of the personal development story is necessarily short. Maintaining beginner status has little reward.

Neophyte

The Neophyte shifts emphasis to selling-skills development, and a beginning *sense* of what product facts mean.

A Neophyte's classic fact-based selling approach is crushingly shallow. The personal selling *touch* acquired through experience is yet to come.

Intermediate

Customers begin to see the intermediate salesman as a resource, and will return for repeat business. Client-based orientation begins to evolve. Selling competence extends to understanding what the facts mean to a prospect; needs-based selling begins at the intermediate stage.

Attention to a prospect's social style, and adjustment of the salesman's behavior's impact on his communication, becomes routine; consciously developed behaviors useful to the sale process are easily recognizable.

Intermediate Game competence is a comfortable position. It's easy to fall asleep in this snowbank.

But here mediocrity is left for the superior individuals who comprise selling's "A-list"—the Advanced salesmen, and their over-achiever superstar constituency, the GameBreakers. This 20% of The Game's participants dominate, earning 80% of compensation in their field.

With 80% of income earned by The Game's players occupying Beginner, Neophyte, and Intermediate categories, an open road is left to the committed individuals who view top performance as the only acceptable option. These are the individuals everyone turns to when a tough job needs to be done right. And right away:

Advanced

The Advanced salesman communicates a *been there* demeanor attributed to notably successful results. Emphasis on customer relationships, and the behavior expected of counselor status, differentiate the Advanced salesman.

Attracting sophisticated customer prospects is well within the Advanced salesman's capabilities. Holding extensive product and market knowledge, and commanding superior selling expertise, the Advanced salesman is an immediately recognizable resource. A few seek über-select, GameBreaker, status.

GameBreaker

Superiority in every aspect of the profession is held by GameBreakers.

Recognized as an expert, a GameBreaker is mentioned by name in discussions associated with *best in the business*. If GameBreakers were professional athletes, they would be all-star game starters.

GameBreakers hold top-of-the-heap status among income earners—dominant even among the 20% who earn 80% of income. If there were a designation as a GameBreaker, Ben Feldman would have dominated in the manner Michael Jordan and Koby Bryant dominated NBA basketball during their time; LeBron James continuing their legacy.

GameBreakers never doubt how they will go about solving a prospect's need. Adaptation to the circumstance's challenges is accomplished with a Samurai master's competence.

At regular intervals it's useful to ask: *What have I learned? What else do I need to know?* Eventually that mentality, as it did for Ben, becomes an everyday thing. You understand the certain things required to succeed, a few more things to become very good, and a lot more to land on the list of *Who's Who in the Jungle*.

To be sure, there is a discernible hierarchy among players. But there is also clear opportunity for accelerated movement from the bottom to the top.

It may be necessary to modify some of your life's pleasures if they are the ones capable of taking you away from going where you want to go. As example, it's not unusual for someone attracted to making a profession of selling to be in possession of a well-sized ego. If there is need to overcome a degree of aggressiveness, cushioning some of the rough edges will be worth addressing.

The ability to listen—not just hearing the words, but understanding the meaning behind the words—dominates in achieving Game success; it's also among the more challenging skills to acquire.

A first requirement is to temper what can be an overpowering desire to comment on any subject, the urge hopefully fading away as Game maturity evolves.

The contrast between achieving Game success, and Game superiority, is equivalent to the difference between a contest participant, and the winner. There will be those satisfied to just participate, others who aspire to be distinguished. The Game's winners prepare to dominate.

We turn to an equally substantive application—psychology's role in Game Success.

PART FOUR
GAME PSYCHOLOGY

CHAPTER FIFTEEN

Psychology's Defining Role in The Game

Human Tendencies

B asic knowledge of human behaviors' importance to sale-transaction outcomes plays a significant role in Game effectiveness.

Understanding certain universal motivational behaviors, identifying social styles—yours, as well as others'—and learning how
to overcome potentially limiting behaviors, are the subjects of this
section. Addressing personal behavioral needs required of effective
Game participation is a first-order action to be taken.

Legacy behaviors—habitually acquired during the process of
growing up—develop for the most part as a result of environment.
Some may be useful to Game activity; others may need to be discarded,
or at least amended.

Acquiring behaviors needed to be effective at the selling process
will require assessment of which existing behaviors will be useful to
you, which may need to be modified, and which others will need
conscious effort to be developed.

But old habits are more interested in your comfort; little interest given to your purpose. Some, capable of poisoning the well, can aggressively work against your best interests.

Think of habits as regulators. What restrictions do you want on yourself? The phrase "that's just the way I am," gives a certain sanctity to anything you do in the way of habit.

But what if the habit is destructive? Is there any reason to pay mightily for a view or habit you acquired by default, under other circumstances?

Controlling the workings of inclination, turning away from what has until now been second nature, can be difficult—but it can be done. The average emotionally healthy individual is deeply habit-ridden; numerous distinct behaviors carry the individual through a largely predetermined daily pattern of activities.

A first understanding is that we are not responsible for the way we are. But second—and just as important as the first—is an understanding that we are absolutely responsible for the way we behave. The assumption is that, if you have a brain in your head, you can act in any manner you choose.

Human nature indulges strong feelings and impulses. But when behavior is controlled only by impulses, competence ends. Several factors influence anyone's behaviors:

The conscience's role;

The ego's influence;

Self-esteem's effects; and

How the brain processes thoughts and feelings.

All are universal, vary in degree of intensity of influence, and assume significant roles in how circumstances are approached.

The Conscience

For the conscience's role, think character. Also, nun with a ruler. No demagogue was ever more inflexibly attached to their time-honored opinions than the conscience. And rules violations, when offended, stipulate that the conscience will speak up.

It's worthwhile to attempt to gain an understanding of an entity's presence capable of wielding such influence over your personal boundaries. The conscience manages an exclusively-yours system of rules, encompassing every moral and ethical behavioral definition.

A product of anyone's past, the conscience begins as a blank slate. The slate is then written upon by parents, peers, teachers, and the culture in which the individual matures. The subsequently evolved judge enforces moral and emotional boundaries, establishing, often strict, rules to abide by.

Like inheriting the family ghost, the conscience evolves into its own entity—dedicated to just you, holding no influence over anyone else. They have their own judge.

For most, the conscience serves a useful function, establishing moral and ethical boundaries associated with high character standards. But, for the unlucky, an overly strict conscience can be powerfully debilitating, pronouncing guilt without remorse for any infraction.

Just about anyone can identify with the horrific experience of having worked for a person or place where no effort was spared to make life on the job intolerable. Such experiences provide considerable incentive to leave town on the next stage.

Ridding yourself of an uncompromising conscience bent on making life miserable is no different.

You inherit these rules governing your life, but you can rewrite some of them—the ones that hold you off. Life can be considerably more satisfying when a vengeful judge, along with its aggressively restrictive rules, is sent packing.

Anyone who has had a difficult time with unwarranted guilt can find it liberating to rid themselves of a conscience that has terrorized them until now, rendering them ineffective in dealing with stressful conditions the circumstances frequently raise.

From this, the right brain's potentially most sinister occupant, the ego, is better understood.

The Ego

The ego is a wild animal. It needs to be free to serve you, but good sense requires some parts of it be held in check.

Clinical psychologists view the ego in two parts, which occupy two very different spaces in anyone's personal universe: the positive ego, there to support you and your best interests; and the negative ego, the source of a host of personal problems.

The Positive Ego

A fortunate advantage for anyone to have is a positive ego's support. The positive ego can play a decisive role as a driving force behind the ability to achieve, or simply as a requisite to functioning well.

Whether an individual's drive is pursuit of praise, recognition, fame, wealth, certificates of merit, compliments, or notoriety, the basis is desire for some sort of personally-defined fulfillment. Aristotle referred to the need as a "Divine Growth Principle," an innate drive to accomplish, a built-in instinct for pursuit of personal development "to fulfill an individual's highest destiny."

A noble cause. But one with a potentially hard edge. It can overwhelm. Aspirations to achieve a worthwhile goal are of value; it's just that an overly ambitious drive to reach the top holds the potential to become self-destructive. When goal attainment evolves into obsession for exceptional achievement it becomes labeled as neurotic.

To most, having the fortunate advantage of a positive ego, praise received, popularity, affirmation, acceptance, or approval are satisfactory evidence to them of personal worth.

The Negative Ego

The positive ego's evil twin, the negative ego, is easily recognizable as patently dysfunctional, hell-bent on torpedoing any attempt to change any of its favorite habits or behaviors. The negative ego takes as its highest duty subversion of the very process that would be best for its host.

But the negative ego's dysfunction is more easily recognized in others than in yourself. You likely perceive yourself as having fewer flaws than the *real you*. There is good reason; a viewpoint capable of dismissing personal flaws as inconsequential resides in the ego.

The negative ego makes its presence known through a galaxy of socially destructive behaviors: arrogance; conceit; possessiveness; jealousy; need to control; social withdrawal; unspoken resentment; a *need* to be right; hypersensitivity; insensitivity; self-absorption; pettiness; emotional demands and manipulations; urge to argue, criticize, judge, blame, or attack; anger, seeking unconscious revenge for past pain inflicted by ... whoever; rage; physical violence; self-aggrandizement; bragging; need for public approval/acknowledgment ... Any will do.

What may appear as confidence—conceit or arrogance—illustrates the opposite, a negative ego in full control. When the negative ego takes over to rule your life, you are no longer working for yourself; your new boss is a lunatic.

Boasting is a way of denying the presence of an overwhelming lack of self-worth. Conceited, or arrogant, individuals are seldom aware that what they view as projecting strength is actually weakness; defenses used to cover insecurities too unsettling to acknowledge.

It used to be that the negative ego was just seen as a bad actor. But today chronic bad behavior is given a label—a dysfunctional something or other. What message is the mind receiving continuously from the negative ego? Danger! From perceived threats. The emotions generated by that message? Fear and anger.

Like a two-ton rhinoceros taken residence in the family room the negative ego can become an overwhelming presence, feeding on circumstances vibrating with its own kind of negative energy: anger; self-righteousness; pride; irrational fears; petulance; destructiveness; hatred; grief over trivial events; emotional drama; an overly critical nature; vindictiveness; self-pity ...

The negative ego's near single-minded purpose is to provide excuses to fail. Dealing with this beast requires acknowledgment: the negative ego's existence is not in question. Recognition provides the means to put it in its place.

Taming the Ego to Your Benefit

The power of freewill plays an important part in the ability to rid yourself of negative personality traits and tendencies' dominance.

It should be apparent that the negative ego at work, like a wizard behind the curtain, is secretly manipulating your behaviors. An epiphany that should rub you the wrong way.

Consider, does your ego support, or deprive, you? Make you more mobile, or hem you in? Enhance your self-esteem, or diminish it? Enable, or prevent, your Game participation? It's your story; write it as though the *self* you think you are owns it. A good beginning is a declared independence of what may be a considerably destructive entity.

Which side of the ego prevails most often depends on an individual's nature—passive, or assertive. The passive individual is the ego's willing prisoner—*It's been okay so far. Why do I need to change now?*

The assertive individual channels the ego's positive side when habit or behavior modification is required—*What do I need to do? I will do it.*

Expect the task of separating how you see yourself from the *real you* to be challenging. An early objective is to overcome the negative ego's penchant for feeding the mind with destructive preferences. You can't cage the ego entirely without killing it, but leaving an out-of-control ego to come and go as it pleases isn't an option either.

There are no neutral conditions attached to negative behaviors, they are purely destructive to selling competence. The big two, fear and anger, are guilt, consequently anxiety, producers.

Anxiety's Role

Guilt and conflict produce anxiety, an aggressively uncomfortable, stress-produced reaction. But most often no single cause produces anxiety; it's a combination of factors.

Deep-rooted anxiety is a natural part of being human. It's not entirely neurotic, but it is ineradicable, and no amount of therapy can remove it.

Anxious, anguish, and *anxiety* are derived from the Latin verb *angere*—to choke. When anger or fear are suppressed, anxiety is experienced. Athletes sometimes choke for everyone to see. Professional golfers get the *yips* when putting, professional baseball players experience batting slumps, normally-capable quarterbacks toss interceptions when the stakes are highest. All fear-based.

Fear-Based Anxiety

All fear is not bad, healthy fear protects your life. But acting on fear of something incapable of causing you bodily harm is self-destructive.

Real danger is easily defined—you can hurt yourself. Avoiding real danger is rational, perceived danger is irrational. Carryovers from the past, irrational fears, like a free-loading uncle, live on in your thoughts and can be as hard to get rid of.

Irrational fears run an extensive gamut. But, for The Game, the real troublemakers are fears of:

Rejection—being told *no* in any form. With rejection, we fear loss.

Failure—inability to admit a mistake, or the possibility you might not be capable of doing something expected of you.

Being "found out"—the possibility that you aren't as good as others have assumed; you aren't as knowledgeable as you are *supposed to be.*

Choice guilt producers, most irrational fears originate in childhood, becoming rooted in a primal fear of disapproval, and disapproval's resulting feelings of inadequacy. Fears in this area are highly exaggerated; facing up to them, essential.

Irrational fear is a reaction to the mind's assumptions. It can be based on unsupported, wholly imagined, possibilities conjured up from who-knows-what past experiences. But, once identified, continuing to be subject to irrational fear is a pure product of your own making. And all selling fears are of this variety.

These fears are pervasive within normal human experiences. If you feel any of them regularly, you are not unusual. Every neophyte salesman deals with these potentially destructive fears.

As a result of dreading the other person's reaction, fear of failure inhibits behavioral learning. Unless you experience the unpleasant symptoms of screwing up, your brain will stick with its comfortable old models, even when ineffective.

But, whether rational or irrational, the result is the same: the body contracts, the physical side of fear erupts into a heart-pounding, sweaty-palms, dry-mouth, inability-to-think-clearly meltdown.

All thought processes shut down, pushed aside when old habits, and the behaviors that go with them, assume full—emotionally flooded—charge. The otherwise capable you is as effectively neutered as a house cat recently subjected to an unsatisfactory visit to the veterinarian.

Leading to anger.

Anger-Based Anxiety

Anger is one of the conscience's favorite guilt-producers. Chalk punishment of the young for anger outbursts onto the slate. When an adult erupts in a display of anger, feelings of guilt are a not-unusual result.

Developed early, emotional reactions to a circumstance attach to a history, a chronology of events, possibly a single catastrophic event. Having become a permanent fixture, the reaction remains as a carryover default behavior until recognized, and dealt with as irrational.

A considerable amount has been written concerning the mind/body connection—what affects one, influences the other. Stress-caused anxiety affecting the ability to function is apparent. But emotional stress isn't the only anxiety-producing culprit; an atrocious diet has been proven to be a potentially significant source of anxiety.

When diet is the culprit, anxiety can be reduced simply by making a few menu corrections. Dealing with stress-caused anxiety requires a decision: overcome what has until now been a limitation, or determine to live with it.

One additional deciding factor in whether there will be a thoughtful response or a knee-jerk reaction to stressful circumstances is how you feel about yourself—self-esteem.

Self-Esteem

Self-esteem (self-worth, self-respect, self-regard)—an individual's general feelings of their own value—is entirely personal. The question, "How do I feel about who I am?" is answered by the relative presence of self-esteem.

A well-developed self-worth is fundamental to a successful selling career. Both a driving-force and conditional, self-esteem varies considerably from one person to another, and within the same individual, depending on circumstances:

Global self-esteem—who we feel we are—is normally constant. Healthy global self-esteem is supported by an ability to take an introspective look at yourself, and still be accepting of the *real you*.

Truly weak global self-esteem, not to be confused with situational self-esteem, is easily recognized by: feelings of inadequacy; guilt; a sense of unworthiness; feelings of inferiority ...

Situational self-esteem—varies by circumstances, roles played, and events. Individuals with normally healthy global self-esteem may, on occasion due to circumstances, experience a temporary lapse. As an example, it isn't probable to be able to walk into a roomful of unfamiliar faces without feeling concern about what others think of you.

Game beginners with healthy global self-esteem will, with reasonable probability, initially struggle with weakened situational self-esteem. The condition will easily correct itself as successful experience develops.

But low self-esteem types will sometimes compensate for an imagined deficiency by coming on too strong, a behavior worth paying attention to as Game behaviors develop. Little is more objectionable in a transactional interaction than opinionated, argumentative people. Humility is called for—not cringing, or self-effacing, just unpretentious, and honest.

In regard to well-being, it's sensible to focus on what needs doing, rather than simply hoping that a confident, happy outlook will bring good things.

The way you feel when you are *out there* will weigh heavily on how you perform. Place attention on actions needed to take you where you want to go. Building self-esteem, particularly as applied to situational self-esteem, can be considerably accelerated through reference to affirmations.

Self-Esteem through Affirmation

A universal condition is that everyone, without exception, has suffered the pain of rejection, experienced inferiority feelings, or endured some emotional hardship. Most people, no matter how self-assured they may seem, have suffered—possibly continue to suffer—from some degree of self-doubt.

Self-esteem can apply to a particular viewpoint: "I am a good salesman, and happy about that," or "I'm not a sales type, and can't do anything about it." One view, uplifting; the other, defeated. Humility and timidity—one a virtue, the other an illness.

An individual with compromised self-acceptance can develop a positive self-image through achieving worthwhile goals. But, until personal achievement has had its positive affect, affirmations can be a useful substitute.

An affirmation is a positive statement consciously made to, then absorbed by, your right brain. The more emotion put into a thought, the more powerful it will manifest. Emotion propels a thought into reality. Thanks to a few notable characteristics the right brain:

Generates impressions, feelings, and inclinations. When any of that group is endorsed by the left brain it becomes hardwired into the right brain's beliefs, attitudes, and behaviors;

Can be programmed to recognize a particular pattern. Think, driving, poker, or riding a bicycle; and in similar manner

Can be trained to execute skilled responses to specific circumstances. Think, The Game or any athletic skill.

Affirmations support what you expect to accomplish, or how you intend to behave. An affirmation is stated as though the intended behavior or attitude being affirmed is already a part of you. Concentrate on self-worth. It stiffens the backbone.

Self-esteem development through reference to affirmations extends over a few weeks. Repeated reference to affirmations are stated aloud:

"I am always prepared before I contact a prospect."

"I am confident, calm, and collected, capable of dealing with anything the circumstances throw at me."

"I am worthy of success."

"When challenged I remain in complete control."

"My word is definite."

"Others count on me."

A form of affirmation, the *Reciprocal Primal Effect,* is a powerful personal development tool. Thoughts focused on an objective—such as becoming very good at The Game—will transform to the acquisition of behaviors consistent with individuals who are very good at The Game.

This will potentially require reference to tempering what might be a few of your own aggressive behaviors, as well as developing an understanding of how to deal with other, overly-aggressive, personalities.

An affirmation, given repetition, will eventually cajole the right brain into accepting the statement as fact.

Aggressiveness/Feelings of Inferiority

Anyone has in their emotional make-up a certain temperamental fire—a willingness to display aggressive tendencies.

Some quietly aggressive types are unstoppable without appearance of being overbearing, saving their aggressiveness for special occasions. For others, openly-aggressive tendencies stemming from deep-rooted insecurities, aggressiveness seems to accompany them like a motorcycle escort.

Openly-aggressive personalities radiate their inferiority feelings through an array of quirky behaviors:

An insatiable need to talk about themselves.

A committed refusal to admit having made a mistake—an almost impossible ability to say "I was wrong."

A driving need to achieve status—rank, position, social.

An overwhelming need for recognition—striving for prominence, prestige, and power.

A need to be right—prideful people can't endure the thought of failure—whether in an argument, in sports, or any other aspect of their life. They must always be right, must always win, and, most definitely must be in control.

A lust for power—a condition firmly rooted in crushing feelings of weakness. Aggressive people attempt to conceal their insecurities by dominating others.

Hypersensitive feelings—insecure people are chronically thin-skinned. It's normal to occasionally experience hurt feelings, to be otherwise would indicate insensitivity to your own and others' feelings.

But when sensitivity extends to a tendency to take personal affront to any number of perceived infractions, inferiority and insecurity are dominating. The slightest hint of personal affront can devastate, or result in the sort of meltdown attributable to a small child's tantrum.

Superiority complexes—the *prince* or *princess syndrome* inevitably will result in the pain of being dethroned. These narcissists developed their feelings from having received excessive parental praise relating to looks, IQ, or athletic skill as a child, resulting in an insufferable snob.

The Prince or Princess in this instance is identified by a list of self-absorbed characteristics: materialism; self-indulgence; lack of concern for social issues; insistence on reliance on others; a strong sense of self-superiority; unwillingness to accept responsibility for their behavior; imposing nonsense demands on others; desire to be treated as an authority ...

A genuine superiority complex is rare, but when apparent, the individual's opinion of themselves will hold probability to be out of proportion with reality.

Megalomania—not unlike a superiority complex, egotism, conceit, and arrogance begins in early childhood as *infantile megalomania*, a condition developed by small children, feeling they are in control.

In a small child, disruptive; carried into adulthood, it manifests as an often out-of-control bully who chooses to be powerful, rather than charming, and feared, rather than loved. Think politician.

But insecurity for some has its compensations. Psychiatrist Alfred Adler, a Freud disciple, suggested that evidence supports moderate feelings of inferiority are capable of stimulating achievement. High achievers are often *gifted* with an internalized need to prove their competence. The apparent good reason is that some, possessed with the advantage of intellect and creativity, find a positive way to compensate.

Feelings of inferiority are acknowledged to have been a driving force behind many of history's great achievers who experienced the worst feelings of inadequacy, self-doubt, and sense of failure. The problem for this group was knowing they were talented, attractive, gifted, brilliant, or a great achiever was insufficient to compensate for not having achieved more.

Quite an industry has evolved from a quest to understand personal achievement, and what drives it. The number of books dealing with ways people are impacted by their early environment, and how to get over it, would fill the shelves of the most formidable Walmart.

Recognizing that the best of your counterparts are subject to some sense of insecurity, inadequacy, self-doubt or self-rejection supports excellent potential for improving how you cope with your own feelings. An awareness of personal weakness provides opportunity to gain an advantage: tweaking one or two aggressive behaviors can have a profound effect on improving prospects for succeeding at a high level.

Mark Twain, in possible acknowledgment of his own shortcomings, observed "You can't eradicate your disposition, nor any rag of it. You can only put pressure on it, and keep it down and quiet."

Extending beyond basic understandings of where you and your prospects may be coming from, acquaintance with a few other Game essentials—*Fixed Action Patterns*—is useful. An array of psychological studies have formalized a useful understanding of this class of human motivators.

Fixed Action Patterns

Fixed Action Patterns are inherited viewpoints and behaviors holding the ability to produce near universally predictable responses. Interactions with business associates, friends, siblings, spouses, make regular reference to these highly predictable conditions.

But polite manners resist the concept of deliberate use of psychological techniques to influence, bringing to mind *manipulation, motivation, subliminal, high-pressure,* and *hard-sell.*

Not liking the concept of influence, society's members are more inclined toward indignation when the use of psychology to influence them is made apparent. The necessity for subtlety in psychology's Game use needs no additional explanation.

But reference to certain built-in motivators can be highly effective, and should be made a part of how you go about The Game:

Material self-Interest	*Consistency*	*Authority*
Support	*Compliments*	*Liking*
Price and value	*Familiarity*	*Similarity*
Contrast	*Self-perception*	*Scarcity*
Reciprocity	*Social proof*	

For those Elmer Gantrys whose business is to inspire—salesmen, fundraisers, politicians, business leaders, evangelists—the very successful take full advantage of these motivators. And you have made use of several since early in your life.

In no particular order the best of Fixed Action Patterns applied to The Game include:

Material self-interest: *What's in it for me?*

Self-Interest requires no clarification: it's all about, *me*. Every rational human being responds positively to the prospect of getting a *good deal*; more particularly when the good deal satisfies a need. In barely fifty years Walmart built the world's largest retail organization based on the single premise, *Always Low Prices*. Good service combines with quality products sold inexpensively.

Support: *Convince me.*

Sale-transaction success improves considerably when a proposed action is attached to a plausible, compelling reason to act.

Because, followed by an unequivocally supported premise, is a *trigger-feature* to a prospect's more open-minded consideration of your proposal. A particularly good reason isn't even required. Almost any will do.

Price and Value: *High price? It must be good!*

"You get what you pay for." Mercedes, Gucci, Bosch … rely on panache to sell their products. The higher the price, the greater the product's perceived utility. Offer the same product with a different label at a 50% off-price, and the value perception can just as quickly disappear, displaced by the price argument. When *cheap* is the motivator, cheap is never cheap enough.

Contrast: *Your grass is green, but … my grass is greener than your grass.*

Contrasting how one product differs demonstrably from another can markedly influence perception.

In one phase of my selling career I specialized as a commercial real-estate broker in the sale of investment properties. Contrast was one of my most effective tools.

A tour of several alternative properties to review with a prospective investor was set, beginning with the assumed least desirable property and finishing with the property most likely to be of interest.

My reasoning had little to do with an awareness of psychological principles; everything to do with what experience seemed to work most effectively.

Reciprocity: *You scratch my back; I'll scratch yours.*
You may not be consciously aware of reciprocity's power, but unconsciously you are—guilt. Having been provided with a favor the expectation is:

A feeling of obligation to return the favor; or

A concession to be received.

Nearly anyone receiving a favor will go to great lengths to avoid being considered ungrateful, or as a moocher.

Reciprocity is capable of producing a *yes* response to a request that, absent a feeling of indebtedness, may have been refused.

Consistency: *You prefer to do it as you have always done it.*
The need to appear consistent is an effective motivator. Stability, and integrity of behavior are proof of a logical and rational mind. Behavioral inconsistency is associated with indecision and confusion.

Make use of consistency when the objective is to engage, setting up the other person's self-image. "I'm calling you because of who you are"—as an important participant in their industry—will encourage their acting in a manner expected of a superior individual.

Self-image/self-perception

The *Principle of Self-Perception*. Paraphrasing Dale Carnegie "Give someone a reputation, then make them live up to it;" "You're good at what you do, I'm calling you because my product is designed specifically for companies like yours."

Association/social proof: *If everyone's doing it, it must be right!*

"Everyone's doing it." To some, a convincing argument. Social proof can rely on numbers—a lot of people, or a few well-known people, using the product.

Cavett Robert, one of selling history's legendary sales trainers, was succinct: "Since 95% of people are imitators, and only 5% initiators, people are persuaded more by the actions of others than any other proof we can offer."

Liking/personal attraction: *I like you. Maybe we can do business.*

Social scientists refer to a positive opinion projected onto an individual they don't know as the *likeability factor*, or the *halo effect*. The condition results when an individual's positive characteristics, such as appearance or mannerisms, dominate perceptions of how they are viewed.

Among professional salespeople, politicians, evangelists, and fundraisers … the cleverest make exaggerated use of likeability. Think, Bill Clinton and Ronald Reagan.

Some individuals are just naturally likeable; others instantly annoy. Fortunately, several paths lead to likeability: physical attractiveness; familiarity; association. Any can produce a positive effect.

Physical attraction: *A well-known halo effect.*

That it's to your distinct advantage to look and sound your best while engaged in The Game cannot be overstated. Business letters, manners, professional appearance, telephone etiquette, openness … will all play a part in other's perceptions of you.

Positive traits—talent, kindness, honesty, intelligence—are near universally attributed to attractive individuals: con men are often silver-screen handsome; con women, drop-dead beautiful. For the more physically average appearing, a tailored business suit is a productive physical attractiveness enhancement.

Similarity: *"We have a lot in common, don't we?"*

Business relationships are favorably influenced by establishing similarity.

Similarities can be found in: viewpoint; personality characteristics; personal background ('I see your company is based in Dallas, a family member lives just outside Dallas."); lifestyle, or similar likes—sports teams, restaurants, geographic areas.

Compliments: *"Yes, go on, I like what you have to say."*

Just about anyone is influenced by flattery. Not about implying gullibility when someone is trying to be manipulative. But as a rule praise brings a positive response, even when inflated.

Familiarity: *The power of persistence—multiple contacts.*

Through a halo effect variation—the *Mere Exposure Effect*—an individual's attitude toward something or someone can be positively influenced by frequency of exposures to the subject. One of selling's most venerable truths, the power of persistence—multiple contacts with the same prospect—relies on the Mere Exposure Effect.

Scarcity: *"What do you mean I may not be able to get it?"*

"If you don't do it now, you may not be able to do it later."
A variation of the *take-away* close: *This promotion ends today;
tomorrow it won't be available.*

CHAPTER SIXTEEN

Personality Factors Affecting The Game

The Game is conducted within an array of personalities. Similarities may seem apparent from one individual to the next, but are more likely remarkably dissimilar despite appearances.

Reference to personality often describes an individual as *having a winning style,* or i*ntelligent, but doesn't show much enthusiasm.* In those definitions personality is based on superficially observable characteristics: sense of humor, friendliness, social skills, energy, evidence of warmth and caring, and so forth. But this is no psychologist's definition. If it was, Attila the Hun had no personality.

Personality is a product of certain genetic predispositions combined with experiential history. Planted into the *Adaptive Unconscious* early in life, the combination influences how the world is both viewed, and approached.

Attempts to define the ideal sales personality have been universally unsatisfactory. But experience has shown that adequate intelligence is a notably useful position to start from, and individuals in possession of excellent interpersonal characteristics are better equipped to more comfortably progress into a sales role.

How someone gets along socially, responds to others, and the extent persuasive powers to influence others are available to them, provides a natural affinity for developing selling skills. But persuasive capability, if not naturally endowed, can be learned by the less gifted.

A written history of classifying people into personality types began with Hippocrates, who around 400 B.C. made the first known attempt, categorizing people into four types:

Sanguine—a cheerful, easygoing type.

Melancholic—depressed and moody.

Choleric—aggressive and excitable.

Phlegmatic—calm and unresponsive.

Hippocrates' observations apparently still make sense as the labels have survived.

Under its current meaning, to be sanguine is to be comfortable and optimistic; melancholic applies to sadness and depression; phlegmatic describes a person who shows low energy and doesn't say much; while *hot under the collar,* describing a hostile and irritable type, derives from the phrase *hot and under the cholera.*

Since Hippocrates, theories have proliferated in attempts to typecast individuals into identifiable categories, everyone fitting into the category said to be of a particular personality type.

Some of those identified include: authoritarian, submissive, introverted, extroverted, stable, neurotic, self-actualized, moral, Machiavellian, masculine, feminine … and plenty more.

The problem is that people don't definitively fit into neatly defined stereotypes.

The quest to define personality has been pursued relatively heatedly during the past century by a few high-profile theorists, including Freud, Nietzsche, Pavlov … and more than a few lesser known, but nevertheless groundbreaking, researchers. Universal to these studies is an understanding—everyone is psychologically hardwired; as a result likely to respond to certain circumstances in reasonably predictable ways.

Behaviorists, specialists who study personality tendencies, consider a variety of personality-related factors. Contemporary personality descriptions popularly focus on five traits common to everyone, regardless of national origin, ethnicity, or gender. Providing a reasonably stable representation of personality, they are in such wide use they have been given a title: the *Big Five*, or the *Five-Factor Model*.

The Five-Factor Model

The Five-Factor Model references—*Openness, Conscientiousness, Extroversion, Agreeableness*, and *Neuroticism*—as disclosing a lot of what we might want to know about someone.

Is a person: extroverted, or introverted? Agreeable, or difficult? Conscientious, or irresponsible? Emotionally stable, or unstable? Smart, or lacking intelligence?

The agreed-upon meanings are generally defined as:

Openness

Openness, under this definition, references whether an individual tends toward analytical thought, or is more inclined to respond emotionally:

Open Types

Open relates to original thinking. Imaginative, right-brain-oriented people are inclined toward esoteric thought, nuances, subtleties, and intellectual curiosity.

Open types express greater appreciation for the arts, exhibit sensitivity to beauty, and are generally more creative. Exhibiting a heightened awareness of how they feel about things, open types are more inclined toward unconventional beliefs.

Characteristically, open types are: full of ideas; quick to understand things; likely to have an extensive vocabulary; fully possessed of a rich imagination; a generator of sometimes profound ideas; and likely to spend time in reflection on the state of things.

Closed Types

At the other end of the Openness spectrum the more closed, down-to-earth conventional type, prefers the plain, the straightforward, the obvious ...

These left-brainers are: less inclined to regard the arts, or even sciences, as having much practical value; not likely to have much of a facility for understanding ideas in the abstract; and not possessed of much imagination.

Closed types prefer familiarity, are conservative in viewpoint, likely to be grudgingly resistant to change, and can just as well be seen as boring.

Conscientiousness

Conscientiousness refers to organization, thoroughness, planfulness ... Achievement begins here.

Conscientiousness influences how impulses are controlled; self-discipline lies in conscientiousness. The conscientious individual's behavior is more typically planned than spontaneous.

Conscientious types avoid trouble. Aiming high for achievement, notable success is acquired through persistence and purposeful planning. Conscientious individuals are often seen as intelligent and reliable; in the extreme may be viewed as perfectionists or workaholics.

Nearly always meticulously prepared, conscientious types are: detail-oriented; exacting in their work; live by schedules; quick to get into projects, then complete them properly; almost never shirk their duties; and avoid leaving things in disarray.

No need to define the other end of the conscientiousness scale's opposites. These Oscars' random behaviors bear little resemblance to any of the conscientious type's precision. Their workspace may just as well appear to have been arranged by a leaf blower.

Extroversion

Extroversion tendencies are readily apparent: positive outlook, energetic, assertive, a penchant for seeking the stimulation and enjoyment of others' company. Clearly engaged with their surroundings, extroverts enjoy being with people. Typically enthusiastic, extroverts are action-oriented, often characterized as *full of energy*, and likely to exude a *let's just do it!* attitude.

The introvert tends to be quiet, more low key, deliberate, less socially involved. Lack of social involvement is not necessarily a result of shyness, but rather a preference for more time alone, and less need for stimulation than extroverts require.

At the outside edges of the extroversion scale:

Extroverts

Enjoy being the center of attention, tending toward being the life of the party;

Feel completely comfortable in a social situation, readily starting a conversation with a stranger;

Will talk to a cross-section of people at a social event.

Introverts

Tend to be quiet around strangers;

Avoid drawing attention to themselves;

Don't feel the need to talk a lot;

Are perfectly comfortable spending time alone.

Agreeableness

Agreeable individuals prefer to get along with others, are generally considerate, friendly, generous, helpful, willing to compromise to accommodate others, and tend toward an optimistic view.

Disagreeable types tend to maintain a suspicious, even antagonistic, world view. The real-hair-shirt variety almost never loses a conversation.

Typically unconcerned with others' well-being, they are less likely to extend themselves to get along. Others' motives can be cause for suspicion, resulting in an unfriendly, hostile style.

Comparing the two extremes:

Agreeable Types	*Disagreeable Types*
Are interested in people;	Are not particularly interested in other people's problems;
Have empathy toward other's feelings; Can be described as *soft-hearted*;	Feel little concern for others, more probably not really interested in people at all;
Generally make people feel at ease; Will take time out for others.	Can be as satisfied as not with insulting others.

Neuroticism

Neuroticism refers to *emotional instability:*

High-scoring types on the neurotic scale are: hot reactors, extremely vulnerable to stress lighting their fuse, coming at you like very angry people.

Neurotics have a penchant for interpreting ordinary circumstances as threatening, and minor frustrations as hopelessly overwhelming.

The typical neurotic's domain is easily disturbed, characterized by frequent mood changes, easily irritated, easily stressed out, often feeling blue, worried about things, even things not likely to happen, but could.

Individuals subject to neurotic extremes live in a near perpetually agitated state, frequently in a bad mood as their negative emotional reactions to perceived slights—anger, anxiety, depression, fear—tend to persist for extended periods.

Low neuroticism scorers are: less easily upset; less emotionally reactive; tend to be calm; emotionally stable; free from persistent negative feelings (most of the time); more relaxed; seldom feel blue; don't spend a lot of energy on worry; and most definitely are planted squarely in the moment.

Freedom from negative feelings doesn't necessarily mean the low neuroticism scorer is overwhelmed by a lot of positive feelings. Those are the extrovert's domain.

Big Five characteristics are not answered in definitive either/or responses. Each characteristic acts independently, and extends through a range of dimensions.

Other testing measures include *temperament* and *mental orientation* traits. Temperament traits consider how an individual might deal with stress or conflict—nervous, anxious, impulsive, or excitable. Character traits consider honesty, morality, and how scrupulous someone tends to be.

Other personality aspects psychologists prefer to delve into—motivations, attitudes, self-concepts, social roles, memories, and life experiences—are not so readily defined.

Mental orientation, the way people think and what they think about, is often measured when individuals are trying to select a job or profession best suited to their temperament and personality.

One widely-used vocational-choice test focuses on a person's preferences—for dealing with people versus things, working with data and facts, or preferring ideas and theory.

Intelligence tests have evolved similarly, measuring a range of mental capacities: vocabulary, mathematics, problem solving, reading ability, creative thinking, memory, and general knowledge.

Traits Most Suitable to Game Participation

Assumed important characteristics concerning the temperament best-suited to a selling career focus on interpersonal traits: how an individual gets along in the social world, responds to people, their willingness to make use of coercion, or a tendency to manipulate other's behaviors.

Some characteristics, like intensity, basic intelligence, integrity, and energy, are inherent to the individual. But some other needed characteristics—confidence, communication skills, sense of humor, and leadership skills—have been learned, or can be learned. It's clear that acquiring a more forceful personality can be developed.

But with that, given no clearly objective measure is possible, Big Five personality traits dominate. Three reasonably distinct qualities—characteristics forming the substance of a sales *person-ality*—seem pervasive among salesmen achieving dominance:

Openness—selling skill relies on creativity associated with more open characteristics. When a more complex sale is on the line, a creatively framed main idea may be the ingredient that makes the sale.

Conscientiousness—for the very conscientious, a well-developed discipline combined with perseverance, are formidable attributes to possess.

Agreeableness—contrary to the fun-to-be-with image of a sales personality, a certain tempering of agreeableness is requisite to Game success. Individuals who do well at The Game are not in need of pleasing when circumstances call for assertiveness in response to an objection, or to close a sale.

Big Five influence is readily apparent in a few tendencies attributed to *social styles* encountered in routine activities.

Recognizing Social Styles

A formidable selling advantage to develop is knowledge of human behavioral tendencies—why you and your prospects respond to circumstances with reasonable predictability.

The condition was disclosed in an early 1960s study conducted by industrial psychologists Roger H. Reid and John W. Merrill, and summarized in their book "Personal Styles & Effective Performance."

Certain behavioral characteristics capable of predicting how an individual might react to circumstances were revealed. How an individual displays emotion, and their intensity of assertiveness, play considerably important roles in how other people see them, how they see others, and how everyday life is approached.

From early childhood the mind, through an array of experiences, develops a potent set of instinctive responses—some sympathetic to others, some not so accommodating. The effect explains why, at the extremes, some people are guided by highly active sympathetic reins while others show little interest in others' feelings.

A variety of factors frame how we see things, and how we go about life, but some dominate. Reid and Merrill concluded two essential characteristics combine to predict certain reasonably apparent behavioral tendencies:

Intensity of assertiveness—how quickly someone gets to the point; how forceful their behavior. Or, how slowly they arrive at a decision, and how much emphasis is placed on facts and careful thought?

Emotional response—how emotion is displayed: cool and aloof? Warm and friendly?

Those behaviors combine to define certain social styles, referred to by Reid and Merrill as: *Drivers, Expressives, Amiables,* and *Analyticals.* Two of these types—Drivers and Expressives—tend toward impulsiveness, potentially combustible, instinctively irreverent; the other two, more careful, leaning toward the precise, the poetry to the other's prose.

It's almost not possible to describe someone without reference to those characteristics, the four types identified as:

Driver	Expressive
High intensity of assertiveness	High intensity of assertiveness
Low emotional involvement	High emotional involvement
Amiable	**Analytical**
Low intensity of assertiveness	Low Intensity of assertiveness
High emotional involvement	Low emotional involvement

An individual's social style doesn't change, disappear for stretches, or show up only in certain words or phrases. It does suggest how an individual exhibiting certain habitual, often readily apparent, behaviors typical of a particular style, is likely to approach their activities:

Driver

Drivers can be daring, nearly always competitive, dynamic, highly assertive, bottom-liners, action-oriented, telling others how-it-is.

Often intensely belligerent, the Driver is direct, to the point, showing little warmth or friendliness: Arnold Schwarzenegger as The Terminator; Donald Trump. Ask a Driver for the time of day and you will get a clear, take-it-or-leave-it response: *It's 3:15!* Case closed.

Drivers are often quick talkers and thinkers, exhibiting an ostentatious *out-of-my-way* style. They can be temperamental and changeable, stubborn and contentious. Coming across as domineering, passionate, driven, narcissistic, the Driver's motivations often include controlling their environment, establishing their authority, and asserting their expertise.

It's an axiom that a Driver can do no wrong. When something is amiss it's the undeniable fault of someone else, who will likely be berated with inspiring zeal.

Drivers will likely not recognize the speed at which they come to a decision. That impersonal characteristic can cause people who disagreed with a decision in the first place, or the pace they have to follow to implement the decision in the second place, to think that the Driver doesn't care about them.

But the Driver is just acting on instinct, "I know what we need to do, let's get on with it!" He's involved in what he's doing and expects everyone else to be involved. By osmosis.

Expressive

The Expressive is *Driver-Light*. Equal parts intensity and fun-loving, the Expressive can be complimentary, diplomatic, unfailingly polite—or a terror.

Illustrating an assertive self-certain style, but adding a lighter touch—David Letterman had warmth and friendliness, and would talk about his personal life. He enjoyed a laugh, but also always controlled the timing and pace of his show. His time-of-day answer might be a flip "Time to do something else."

Often the motivator, the Expressive is the best speaker from the platform, the master of ceremonies, the inspirational type who puts stories together about people, their successes, their relationships, tugs at your heartstrings, makes you feel the story … You cry, laugh, cheer, clap, or wave the flag—everything most people associate with the idea of motivation. Presidents Reagan, and Clinton were flaming Expressives.

Amiable

Amiables are all warmth and friendliness. Mr. Rogers wants to be your friend, and move into your neighborhood.

Amiables excel at reading social cues, quickly appeasing someone else's apparent stress, and figuring how to make the other person feel important. Those interests are self-serving; Amiables have a need to keep others on their side.

The Amiable is patient, careful, and prefers working as a team member. Placed into leadership positions, they are consensus builders. Emphasizing, and capitalizing on, relationships, Amiables look for approval: "Tell me I am right." "Tell me you appreciate my work." "You like me. You really, really like me."

Asked for the time of day, the Amiable might respond with: "What time would you like it to be?"

Analytical

The Analytical, as stubborn as the Driver is forceful, tends toward being more serious, and loves (actually lives for) detail. Analyticals are reliable; you can depend on them. The Analytical's time of day response: "Let me look into it; I'll get back to you (just don't push me)."

In direct contrast with the Expressive's, or Driver's grand sweep the Analytical does his work with a thoroughness revering detail as a near religious experience.

Physically an Analytical is likely to be rather poker-faced, not much animation, a vice president of finance, a tax lawyer … What the Analytical lacks in flash is compensated for by substance.

Each style has its strengths. Personal success is not a strict function of social style, but some roles are better suited to one style than another. Picture Arnold Schwarzenegger's Terminator replaced by

Woody Allen; Mr. Rogers as the Tonight Show host. Those people are, or were, successful in careers considerably defined by their clearly apparent social styles.

Anyone can consciously control their habitual tendencies to suit particular social or business interactions. But short of conscious control, their social style will make their actions generally predictable, more particularly when there is some stress—as in a sale transaction.

An individual's social style will indicate something of how they will likely respond. The condition leads to a readily apparent Game advantage: when you understand your style, identify the other person's style, then adapt your behavior to suit their likely preferences your ability to influence takes a considerable upward turn.

It's sensible to pry into how a few of your behaviors affect others' responses to you. Becoming adept at dealing with each social style's probable behaviors and preferences will be easier with adjustments made in your approach to each.

CHAPTER SEVENTEEN

Essentials of Thought Processing and Remembering

Thought and Emotion

Thought drives emotion—yours and your prospect's. An understanding essential to Game participation is:

It isn't circumstances that cause you trouble; only your thoughts give them meaning; and

You can frame a presentation's main idea to engage a prospect's thoughts, consequently positive emotional responses. A prospect will not remember everything you said. But they *will* remember what they felt.

The neuroscientific community has determined that people tend to have one of two thinking styles:

The first, Analytical—logical, and mathematical, often attributed to be controlled by the brain's left hemisphere;

The Second, Intuitive—attributed to the brain's right hemisphere, feelings-oriented, artistic, creative, musical, and emotional.

These predispositions are referred to as *cognitive styles;* one or the other will dominate from one individual to the next.

As to the left-brain/right-brain concept, it's true that physically the brain is composed of two halves, but reference to left-brain/right-brain orientation is only metaphorical.

Brain locations where feelings reside—performing the functions attributable to the right-brain process—are made up of several components, referred to by author Stephen King as "the boys in the back room," and by psychologists as the *Adaptive Unconscious.*

Conscious ("left-brain") thinking is performed by the *Prefrontal Cortex,* which overlaps the brain's two halves like a canopy.

But continuing with the left-brain/right-brain concept:

Left-brain thinking focuses on the literal, the facts. Conscious thought, centered in the Prefrontal Cortex, guides discussion;

Right-brain activity is about feelings. Right-brain functions are pre-wired, acting without need for, or interference from, the Prefrontal Cortex's participation.

During rapidly evolving conditions, thought and feelings combine to make sense of the circumstances:

First, the process Analytical and Amiable types are most familiar with: "Let me think it over and get back to you with a good answer." Logical, literal, deliberate, sensible ... Facts considered; an answer formulated.

In the second, without conscious recognition, intuition takes over: the problem's solution, near instantaneous. A process referred to by cognitive psychologists Gerd Gigerenzer, and Peter M. Todd, as fast *and frugal* in their book "Fast and Frugal Heuristics: The Adaptive Toolbox." It's how gut conclusions are reached.

Most of the time, thanks to the Adaptive Unconscious, activities that would otherwise require conscious thought are on cruise control. The most ordinary variables, none requiring conscious attention, processed with the ease of a stroll in the park.

The mind's normal state is to have intuitive feelings and opinions, the Adaptive Unconscious serving as a virtual filter, informally, *gut feeling*. "Do I trust this person?" "Am I willing to accept what I am hearing?" A selling presentation's appeal to emotions supports another of selling's oldest premises: gut feeling drives buying decisions—and selling behaviors.

When there is no time to stop and ponder a decision, the Adaptive Unconscious sizes up the circumstances, identifies the problem, and takes action. Acting as a light-speed computer, the Adaptive Unconscious quietly processed what would otherwise have been an overwhelming volume of data, and arrived at a conclusion.

It isn't possible to explain the mechanism for detecting a hint of irritation in a telephone voice, or how a sudden traffic event was avoided before you were consciously aware. But the right brain picked up on both, and acted.

It's from an indefinable edginess, a right-brain ability to assess circumstances and proceed without total information necessarily being available.

In basketball the player who can comprehend the chaos around him is said to have *court sense*, a football quarterback has *field sense*. Generals possess *power of the glance*, the ability to see and make instant sense of a battlefield, lightening quick action taken based on a well-developed gut instinct.

Mastering any developed skill relies on the Adaptive Unconscious' stored behaviors. When The Game is on the Adaptive Unconscious' version of court sense separates one participant's competence from others. Habitual behaviors, essential to responding when circumstances require, reside here.

The Adaptive Unconscious, keeping tabs on details, constantly determines appropriate actions. Anyone, with rush-hour traffic coming from all sides, can relate to thinking through available alternatives among the volume of information their brain is receiving.

Playing any sport would be chaotic, and anyone would be helpless under selling conditions, if sense could not be made of complex situations in a flash. But there is a catch: how well decisions are made under high-stress conditions depends on behaviors specific to, and developed for, the event. Potentially negative legacy behaviors are modified, or replaced.

In attributing value to analytic versus intuitive decision-making, neither is better than the other. Both have value under the right conditions. What is not good is when one process dominates under the wrong circumstances.

It would be a rare human being who has not avoided telling someone to go to hell when circumstances are screaming for a satisfying, if poorly-timed, response of a similar kind to the moment's preferences.

In such moments the more level-headed left brain steps in and trumps the sometimes volatile right brain's desire to let-it-fly. Charged with remaining polite when at your wits end, the sensible left brain assumes control, and saves what might otherwise have been a take-no-prisoners reaction.

But the conscious process, while thoughtful, has its limitations. It's slow; it needs information. When intuitive judgment is the pre-emptive of-the-moment, definitely in-your-face, need—the business end of a junkyard dog is seeking your acquaintance—time for deliberation is limited.

The right brain's drawback is that it operates entirely on its own. Instead of deliberation over the facts, the right brain, through sweaty palms, dry mouth, urge to run, or fight, senses, "We have some stress here." Intuitive conclusions are reached well before conscious awareness of the action to be taken is reached.

While conscious thought is considering which horse to bet on, the Adaptive Unconscious has completed a series of instant calculations; conclusions reached, the horse let out of the gate.

The process is sudden, and when acting on faulty notions can be inappropriate. That nuance is the fast and frugal process' drawback. Also its opportunity.

Beyond the conscious part in how you go about your activities, or your viewpoints related to rights and wrongs, the right brain is taking in others' actions. Is this person: Talkative? Likely to find fault with others? Thorough? Original? Reserved? Flippant? A complainer? Argumentative? A crashing bore? ...

Conscious attention given to the development of desirable behaviors to be placed into the Adaptive Unconscious will be to your distinct advantage in perfecting Game outcomes.

One such dominating behavior is communication—understanding yours, and your customers'.

PART FIVE

GAME COMMUNICATION

CHAPTER EIGHTEEN

Communication's Game Dominance

Communication and The Game

Game substance has no more positive advantage to develop than a powerful communication style. If a professional salesman were a warrior, his skill would be communication; his sword, spoken words and nonverbal communication.

Can you put together a unique combination of absolutely compelling words? For most, this is improbable. But the potential to make improvements, some remarkable, is there for everyone.

Look around you. Observe the most effective individuals. Consider their communication competence as a benchmark.

Given a choice between someone who really knows his facts, and a capable communicator of what the relevant facts mean, the communicator will dominate. Communication skill extends beyond command of language, to how a thought is expressed, powers of observation, assertiveness, and a well-tuned response to others' behavioral cues.

The difference in skill between most people and those recognized as outstanding communicators (former Presidents Clinton and

Reagan, Billy Graham) can be considerable. People recognized as motivational types leave verbal footprints when they speak. Like theater actors, they bring words to life.

But it's only *somewhat better* distinguishing a professional salesman from others whose communication may leave them near constantly at odds with of-the-moment circumstances.

Communication is a composite—an infinite variety of combinations: word selection, speech inflection, pauses, rate of speaking, listening skill, and nonverbal actions. Spoken communication is expressed verbally, and non-verbally (everything but the words)—nonverbal communication dominating.

Communication professionals place relative importance on spoken communication categories as: non-verbal, 65-70%; tone of voice, 25-30%; words, five to 10%.

Conversational speech rate is generally acknowledged as 110 - 150 words per minute. In some places, like New York City, people tend to naturally speak faster, while in the Southeast people are inclined to speak more slowly.

But natural speech is capable of speeding up, or slowing down, depending on circumstances. We speak more rapidly when we're in a hurry, saying something urgent, or trying not to be interrupted. For most people, nervousness or excitement will increase their rate of speech.

In ordinary conversation, without conscious awareness, you respond to thousands of nonverbal communications every day. Body posture, tone of voice, facial expressions, eye gaze, gestures, clothing, tattoos/face metal, handshake, hairstyle … all tell something of the individual, and affect how they and their communication's content will be perceived.

Sale Communication

Clear communication—spoken, or written—is concise, always direct.

Sale-transaction communication can be simple or made complex; the standard can be positive or torpedoed by an array of potent self-inflicted barriers, two of the most notable being:

Poor listening—not really hearing what the other person is *truly* communicating. What was heard was not what was intended; and

Compromised personal communication skills—what *your* behavior is actually communicating, when the intent was otherwise.

Obstacles compromising communication are removed by directing attention from what you plan to say, to how the other person is responding. Communication can assume any of several forms:

Disinterested—no direct involvement, listening is passive. There may be good reason. You may simply have little to say, or are listening to someone who has little to say, but insists on saying it anyway.

To that point, no problem. But save disinterest for occasions when consequences are of less concern than those that apply to a sales call.

Participative—participative conversation is random, no point required, a conversation with a friend over what time to meet, last night's basketball game …

Counselor—the counselor's role is definite: understanding the other person's *real* communication. Beyond just hearing, the counselor *feels* what the other person is saying. When the conversational ball is tossed to the counselor, response is in perfect sync.

Participative conversation is free-form, laced with a lot of personal agenda. The counselor's communication appears free-form, but knows exactly where the discussion needs to go. And goes there.

Engaging Different Social Styles

A sale transaction's first objective is to arouse the prospect's enthusiasm—*yes, I'm interested*—or to conclude the prospect has no need for the product.

The strategy behind the objective depends on how what is to be communicated is delivered. The *how* adjusts to the prospect's social style.

Behaviorists refer to an interaction between two people as a *transaction.* A sale transaction begins with determining how the other is most likely to respond to your approach.

Amiable and Analytical types carefully work their way through things; Drivers and Analyticals are more likely to skip the social niceties and get straight to the point.

Expressives are inclined to get to the point, but will add some feelings into the event. Amiable types are driven by feelings, but inclined to be slow to arrive at a decision.

Adjusting your behavior to accommodate a prospect's preferences makes sense. Are they a bottom-liner, requiring that you get to the point? Do they need some detail? More inclined toward an open friendly style?

Even casual accommodation of each social style's tendencies will elevate ability to influence immensely when your behavior results from your having made a conscious choice based on the prospect's probable preference.

When interacting with each style:

The Driver: *Dealing with a Driver? Get on with it. Lights! Action!*

In dealing with Drivers, their probable motivation will be to control the circumstances, establish their authority, possibly assert their own expertise. Emphasize your understanding of the Driver's, or the Driver's company's, reputation, their high standards, and how your product serves their interests.

A Driver's controlling behavior originates in the belief that others are not possessed of their discipline or high standards. By relentlessly monitoring and needling people, Drivers are convinced they can force others to conform to their way of doing things.

In their relations with you, impersonal. The Driver's not looking to be your buddy. The relationship, strictly business.

A relationship might come later if the task is accomplished to the Driver's satisfaction. The condition can be a problem for an Amiable, who, needing strokes to confirm how well accepted he is, tries to cozy up to a Driver. That foray into the land of really poor judgment can only turn the circumstances dark.

Driven by the belief their approaches to dealing with problems produce the best results, Drivers will attempt to control your presentation's timing, and will challenge your premise.

The Driver excels in circumstances requiring quick decision-making, getting straight to the point. Not easily persuaded by just facts, Drivers will live up to their style, "Why should I spend time on this?"

Drivers make it clear their respect must be earned by others' willingness to perform at their exacting level. Let Drivers know that you understand their need to have things *done right,* that you have the resources to meet their standards.

A Driver will respond to such statements as "We will achieve for you ..." "What this means is ..." The Driver's bottom-liner language preferences include words such as *authority, require,* and *need.* The Driver gets to the point: "I will do this, if you will do that." Avoid any appearance of waffling in your responses.

When a Driver's decision is reached, it can be made with the finality of a chiseled-in-marble commandment sent down from the Mount.

The Expressive: "*Let's get to the point, but let's have some fun while we're at it.*"

The Expressive, while one part intensity, is also another part fun, more probably attaching feelings to circumstances that the Driver does not. Expressives are inclined to be good listeners, and more agreeable to consider your premise.

Influence Expressives with such words as *needs* and *benefits.* As a bottom-liner the Expressive is action-oriented, fast-paced, nervy, inspirational, passionate, and inclined to lose patience with the more laborious mind that does not instantly agree. But he can be sold, if quickly engaged.

Emphasize your respect for the Expressive's company's excellent reputation; how the opportunity to speak with them is appreciated. Expressives respond to a certain amount of panache; word pictures are particularly useful.

There may be the occasion when, focused on how your idea will enhance their future, a tent evangelist's enthusiasm may work well.

The Analytical: "*My conclusions stand on their own merits.*"

Among alternatives, Analytical's may accept only the best, assuring themselves that a decision made was the gold-standard among all possible options.

By nature cautious, at times downright skeptical, you don't toss quick answers at an Analytical's objections. The Analytical needs to understand your complete agreement of the need to work through a logical answer to a problem before you are comfortable in doing anything about it.

Analyticals need to be shown, responding best when you sound like an accountant. When you respond to a question with "Let me get back to you on that," the Analytical sees someone who understands the value of doing things right.

Likely to be withdrawn from a personal relationship, you don't get cozy with an Analytical without having your tail-feathers singed. That sort of attempt holds excellent potential to result in an Analytical concluding "I'm not so sure about this person."

The Analytical is most likely to respond best to facts, and proof: "It's apparent more detail is required. I will see to it." "We are the market leader for a reason." "Key factors in the market, A, B, and C, all make use of our product."

When appropriate, include facts and statistics to back your statements, emphasized by such terms as *evidence, logic, the facts show, based on the data.*

Even if your notes are jotted onto the back of an envelope after leaving an Analytical's office, a carefully prepared analysis set on his desk at the next meeting will impress. Your behavior will have been deemed—credible.

An Analytical's concerns will include "never having done that before," and with making a mistake. Analyticals need validation. What is being proposed has proven successful for others; they will not be made to look foolish if they buy into what you have to say.

The Analytical is slow to arrive at a decision, stolid, maddeningly conscientious. No proposal too lengthy or too complex for an Analytical to scrutinize down to the last punctuation mark. Just as bottom-liner (Driver and Expressive) types avoid trivia, the Analytical devours it.

The Amiable: *To an Amiable, continuity and security are synonymous.*

Dealing with an Amiable? You are the politician. "What would you like to hear? And how would you like to hear it?" The Amiable works from feelings, is likely to use phrases such as "I know what you mean"; "Tell me more"; "What do other people think?"

People-oriented, indirect, optimistic, not given to impulsiveness, Amiables are inclined to be good listeners, respectful, polite, and likely to be amenable to a reasonable premise. Emphasize your company's market reputation, and your appreciation for speaking with them.

Amiables, like Analyticals, can be more cautious in their decision-making, and slower to get off dead-center. Characteristically masters of circuitous solutions to problems, Amiables are less likely to be forceful in their views early in the discussion, but can be forceful later when circumstances require.

A consensus builder, often the Amiable's attempt is not to prove a point or to advance a proposal, but to gain others' approval.

Discussion with an Amiable may require engaging in small talk, letting them explain how they feel, soliciting their support. When feeling unsure, the Amiable is likely to throw in such concerns as "We've never done that before," or "The mistake would be ..." Your response: "You may be familiar with others who have proven the service's value to their business." The communication: the idea is not radical, or overly risky.

Like Analyticals, Amiables are slower to change direction. An aggressive attempt to force a decision from an Amiable holds probability to end badly. Crossing that line in a sale transaction may set off explosions of anger. But short of that the Amiable will remain endlessly polite and accommodating.

When dealing with Analyticals or Amiables, understand that either is likely to:

Require more information than bottom-liners to reach a decision;

Continue the evaluation process even after a decision has been reached;

Take longer than bottom-liners to make a decision;

Place more emphasis than bottom-liners on comparing their decisions to other options;

Experience regret—*buyer's (or seller's) remorse*—after making a decision;

Think more about hypothetical (as opposed to real) alternatives to a purchase they have made; and

Remain skeptical about their decision.

You know them all. People who can choose quickly and decisively, others who agonize over every detail as a major event. What is certain is each social type is a prisoner of their own nature. Two are immovable objects; the others, an irresistible force. When the two contrasts interact there will be some heat.

Picture Mr. Expressive's all-energy, out-there style—Brioni suit, alligator shoes, designer tie—blasting into the Analytical's office. The scene: the Analytical seated behind a desk devoid of any papers other than the file being immediately addressed. The dress: gray pin-striped suit, white shirt, and suitably conservative tie. You can just imagine the Analytical's frantic search for a place to duck and hide.

A bottom-liner's role as a salesman can use some help by slowing down when approaching strangers. Coming on too strong will near certainly place an Expressive or a Driver at instant odds with an Analytical or Amiable.

Reversing the circumstances, the Analytical arrives at the Driver's office hyper-prepared. A properly detailed proposal, fully tabulated and footnoted. The Driver's unblinking gaze fixed on Mr. über-prepared tells the story, "You have 30 seconds to convince me why I should waste another moment with you." Bottom line, get to the point.

The Analytical, keeping his composure, says "These facts prove I can save you 25% in your costs, all of it dropping to the bottom line. I will discuss the details with your accounting manager. Here is a *Reader's Digest* version of the facts." The Driver is now sitting forward in his chair.

Don't expect praise from Drivers or Analyticals for your excellent work. Your A+ performance simply meets their everyday expectations. But since neither rarely gets much appreciation from others, a little acknowledgment of their perfectionist standards can go a long way.

Bottom-liners often see *good enough,* as being just fine. Worry about the possibility that there may be something better? No need. It doesn't mean a Driver or an Expressive doesn't have standards. Just that when the standard is met the search is over. Potential for a better option around the corner is not of concern.

Understanding social-style preferences supports communicating the impression you intend. But, regardless of how accommodation is made to any style, there will be stress in a sale transaction resulting from your:

Purpose—to sell them something they assume they *don't need,* and *isn't in the budget;*

State of mind—possibly nonverbal stress that the other person picked up on; or

Two styles clashing—the turtle and the hare. The Expressive or Driver can be just too fast for the Analytical or the Amiable who need time to ponder the facts; the Amiable or Analytical can be too tedious for the Driver's or the Expressive's "Just give it to me straight" viewpoint.

So should there be an attempt to eliminate stress from the discussion? Not possible. Stress is an unavoidable Game component. But by controlling your behavior:

The other person's trust and confidence in you and what you have to say, can be gained; and

With that, their willingness to work with you; and

From there, you can move on to determining what they would like to do; then

It's possible to assist them in getting there.

It's a product of your behavior.

Communication Disclosure— The Value of Opening Up

Beyond preferred social style, an individual's thought-disclosure tendency, *open* or *closed,* can profoundly affect a communication's result.

Everyone has open/closed tendencies, influenced by circumstances, but habitually tend toward one or the other—more open, stating what's on their mind; or more closed, keeping their cards close. The two extremes typically illustrate tendencies as:

Closed communicators edit their words carefully. Self-protection overrides communication—"what you don't know about me you can't use against me." Thoughts are kept private; questions answered by a short, *yes*, or *no*, or diverted to another subject.

Open communicators are proverbial open-books, the extrovert at his best. You know just about everything happening in their life; possibly more than you care to know.

Open communicators are generally more likeable; more enjoyable to interact with. The communication is they aren't afraid to lower their guard, even to seem a bit corny. The open communicator's manner puts others at ease; you find yourself enjoying watching them in action.

Excluding chronic complainers—individuals who insist on unburdening their full array of problems on anyone available—an open communication style communicates self-confidence.

With likeability a distinct selling advantage, Game effectiveness favors a more open style. Few people are fully open, or resolutely closed. But developing the ability to open up in a sale transaction is worth your attention if your normally preferred style is more closed.

Attaching Presentation Memorability

No matter how objectively a prospect documents their reasoning behind a decision, *gut feeling* will dominate. It just *feels right*. That nuance highlights two errors common to novice salesmen:

Reliance on a data dump or a random form of presentation— presentations focused on product-related facts. What the facts mean, lost in magnificent irrelevance; and

Lack of attention given to the first impression—an initial contact passes through a prospect's very discriminating gate—their right brain filter: "do I want to do business with this person?"

But, even when a first impression is favorable, a presentation focused on facts and figures to make a point lacks emotional attachment.

The prospect has no personal involvement with the product. The gist of one of selling's most venerable truths—conclusions are reached emotionally (*sell the sizzle, not the steak*)—has just been soundly violated.

In contrast the experienced salesman frames, in easily visualized terms, what the facts *mean* to the prospect.

Selling the Sizzle

Gain a prospect's trust through communicating a likeable manner—warm, genuine, open. Your energy and expressiveness will engage the prospect near instantly:

Your prospect has your undivided attention—you are receptive to your prospect's responses; they are open to yours;

When the communication is face-to-face—light it up with eye contact; eye contact is nonverbal punctuation. Just don't overdo it. Too much eye contact can be perceived as overly aggressive;

Things are kept moving—you are fully aware of your prospect's nonverbal responses, actions communicate your enthusiasm, and how your product directly addresses their needs; and

When the discussion is by telephone, emphasize voice quality—make full use of pauses and speech intonation; thoughts not associated with the moment are closed out.

A particular communication grammar—conventions and rules attaching tacitly understood meanings under certain circumstances—is acquired by everyone through their environment. Certain terms acquire generalized meanings, with some not necessarily a dictionary's definition.

Presentation clarity can be supported by an array of communication options extending beyond simply words. Ben Feldman's power phrases made use of the condition—elegantly, or when he felt the necessity, forcefully—supporting salient points through an array of adaptable communicators:

Metaphors—metaphors are analogies: "This will place a considerably improved horse in your race."

Similes—a simile states a *like* condition: "Access to this sort of service is like having a Ferrari in your driveway."

Aphorisms—aphorisms are subjective truths: *you can schedule a fishing trip, but you can't schedule a fish fry.* Sometimes referred to as wisdom literature, aphorisms can be as simple as Ben Franklin's "Time is money," or "A penny saved is a penny earned."

Other familiar aphorisms in contemporary use: *hindsight is 20/20; less is more;* or Thomas Jefferson's "I find the harder I work, the more luck I seem to have."

The difficulty with referencing aphorisms is that many, having evolved into clichés, have lost the value of originality.

Epigrams—epigrams are aphorisms' close cousins. An often satirical statement, the epigram drives straight to the point: Oscar Wilde's "I can resist everything but temptation," or Ralph Waldo Emerson's "What you do speaks so loudly that I cannot hear what you say."

The epigram differentiates from the aphorism by the epigram's sarcastic edginess.

Anecdotes—a story describing a success similar to the prospect's circumstances, "Brigham Residential saved 20% from prior year expenses using this service." Ben Feldman made reference to well-known people who had died without sufficient assets to protect what would otherwise have been a formidable estate from devastating taxes. One example was former President Franklin D. Roosevelt.

Visual aids—with 90% of the population receiving their information visually, have something to show. If the transaction is by telephone, make use of the web to provide visual support. Absent visual support, use word pictures.

Outrageous analogy—to make a point memorable think of it in an outrageous setting—"It's the difference between a bicycle and a Ferrari." "You have a 10-foot ditch, and a six-foot plank."

Appeal to the senses—involve your prospects as they like to be involved. Do they prefer their information in packaged form? Or in sensory language? A steak can be a *12-ounce filet,* or *aged, Kansas City corn-fed beef, seared to perfection; served by candlelight and music.* Add to that someone you enjoy being with. One definition, to the point; the other, engaging the senses. One is sustenance; the other, an experience.

Make use of questions and answers—questions clarify the prospect's perceptions, and needs.

An added bonus to use of epigrams, metaphors, and similes to make a point is the near complete lack of ambiguity. Some word pictures express a point so concisely no further elaboration is required. A few sprinkled strategically into your discussion can make your prospect want to hear more.

But, even when a metaphor or anecdote isn't crystal clear, it can still be close enough that the point will be made.

CHAPTER NINETEEN

The Language of Selling

A selling presentation is a product of the imagination, one creative intelligence interacting with another.

Best delivered in a conversational manner, a presentation differs from a casual conversation in that a presentation has a clearly intended outcome. Communication is concise. Simple, everyday language enhanced by the power phrase.

Certain words or word combinations resonate, communicating strength; others appear weak. No apparent reason applies to why words spoken can have either effect any more than why musical notes in a particular combination are deeply stirring, while the same notes rearranged are fingernails on a chalkboard.

Winston Churchill, one of history's great communicators, said "Short words are best." He finished with, "And old words, when short, are best of all." Mr. Churchill was referring to the written word, but the observation holds for spoken communication.

Poetry, good literature, and notably effective selling make use of metaphors, epigrams, similes, and stories. Ben Feldman, as one of selling history's most definitively successful salesmen, was a master of epigrams to illustrate his premise. Ben never failed to make his point—"You *need* this product." When a sale transaction was on, his personalized power phrase bag was at the ready:

"When you walk out, the money walks in."

"Term insurance is temporary, but your problem is permanent."

"You are already broke, and don't know it."

"Every man has problems that only life insurance can solve. In the young man's case, the problem is to create cash; for the older man, to conserve it."

"Put me on your payroll. The day you walk out, I will walk in and pay your bills."

Ben never wavered in his admonition to others, "Don't sell life insurance. Sell what life insurance can do."

It isn't necessary to be a Ben Feldman to be a very good communicator. Developing a keen awareness of the results of what you are doing can make communication interesting, and memorable.

Word Types

A personal set of grammar rules governing an individual's communication intent is, for the most part, specific, but can occasionally be arbitrary.

Words, particularly certain poetic words, can have a broad variety of meanings. As example, Spring can bring to mind end of Winter, flowers, rain showers, gardening, cool breezes … or simply the season between Winter and Summer.

It's not unusual for commonly used words or word combinations when inserted into a face-to-face transaction or letter, to weaken a thought:

Interesting: if what you are about to state is interesting, skip the preamble. Make it so.

Approximately: a hedge.

Each and every one: a pitchman's jargon.

In terms of: word padding.

One of the most: feeble.

The foreseeable future: a cliché; a devastatingly fuzzy one at that.

The truth is ... The fact is ...: if you are possessed of the truth or the facts, no advance billing is needed.

Utilize: rather than *use.* Why?

Linguists categorize speech nuances into word types:

Descriptive—objective observations are fact-based for recording or transferring data and messages, or referring to things or events. Descriptive terms are used among individuals with working knowledge of a particular activity's word meanings.

Action—motivational types—politicians, trial lawyers, evangelists, army commanders, coaches, business leaders, and high-powered salesmen—have in common an action-oriented, to-the-point, speaking style. Intonation and facial expressions transform words into calls for action.

Action-oriented language incites decisions, encourages participation, and arouses passions. No-nonsense, men-of-action types may resort to the *Ablative Absolute,* speech in pure form used by individuals who don't waste words: "You need a sledge hammer; you have a tack hammer." "You're already broke, and don't know it."

Poetic—poetic language captures a mood.

A scientist can mathematically describe a seashore wind current. But to someone strolling along a beach on a summer evening, a light breeze moving the air, thought given to numeric functions will be improbable.

Poetic language describes sensations, the—serenity of the sea, calm comfort of a wood fire, biting humor of a joke, goose bumps from listening to an emotional musical arrangement ...

Under the right circumstances glorious prose can be impressive. But not in a sale presentation. Prose without a motivating premise, is just verbal bling.

A selling presentation is a well-crafted piece of work, a clearly framed main idea within a story, transporting a prospect along an interesting, potentially inspiring, path.

Passive—many expressions heard in normal conversation are often not so much poor English, as poor style. Words capable of ambushing what might have been an otherwise well-considered presentation include such contributors to weak communication as:

Speech modifiers *(kind of, sort of)*

Hedges *(I think, I feel)*

Fillers *(uh, um,* or *well)*

Overly polite *(please, sir, if you will ...)*

Excuses *(I apologize for not being available, I was ...)*

Conditional language *(would, should, if, could). If* is conditional; *when* implies certainty; something will happen.

Passive communication's sale transaction equivalence is cotton candy's contribution to nutrition. And an elegant vocabulary, while a potentially powerful attribute, can undo an otherwise excellent selling presentation.

Insertion of a few five-dollar words into the conversation is just as capable of weakening communication as insertion of a "his'n," "he don't," or "ain't."

Whether writing or speaking, the active voice is more concise; the positive statement, more motivational. Habitual active-voice use is forceful, a quality capable of extending to statements of any kind.

There are other word usages to avoid—speech anomalies.

Words to Avoid—Speech Anomalies

It would be preferable if others' reactions to what you have to say were responding to intended meaning. But speech anomalies—jargon, poor syntax, use of passive language, or slang—are classic sale call what-not-to-dos.

Speech anomalies are throwaway remarks. Never genuine expressions of thought, all hold the ability to trigger a potentially negative reaction. You may not know them by their descriptive terms, but you do know them:

Poor grammar—*ain't, hisself, theirselves, anyways, leastwise*—are grammar disasters. Any will result in uncomplimentary judgments made about an individual's mental acuity.

Malaprops—malaprops are word substitutes, sounding like they should be right: *is this tent water repellicant?* Or, the widely used, *irregardless.* One of former President George W. Bush's favorite pronunciations was *nucular.* Mr. Bush's word may have been correct, but held the potential to sound less than intelligent.

Obscenities function for:

Verbal abuse;

A signal that you are part of a group in which use of obscenities is a group characteristic. In that instance obscenities are a *register*, a speech form dedicated to use within a defined group; or

For distracting a listener from anything else you have to say.

Epithets—light obscenities, epithets differentiate from full-on, industrial-strength four-letter-word obscenities in that epithets are less formalized. You can make one up: *Dagnabit,* or *You intemperate, indecisive hyper-vegetarian excuse for a ...* Epithets are as efficient as obscenities in distracting a listener from whatever else you may have to say.

Euphemisms—as a substitute for an expression considered offensive or vulgar (i.e. *freaking, wuss, privates, SOB ...*). The problem is they may have acquired the offensive word's same connotation. Avoid euphemisms as you avoid obscenities or epithets in a sale transaction.

Boundary Words and Phrases—boundary words and phrases are slang terms that come into the language for a while, then go. Words and phrases such as *like, you know, well, okay, totally, I mean, awesome, cool, yeah-yeah-yeah* (said machine-gun-like), *amazing.*

> "Well okay, the first thing we should do, okay? is discuss what we have available, know-what-I-mean? Like, if we have something that, you know, may, like, be of interest, then that would be totally awesome."

Boundary terms sweep into the conscious like a fog. As contagious as the flu, they become habitual, and hard to get rid of. Spend time around someone making use of boundary terms and you may find your speech peppered with them.

Clichés—a boundary-phrase cousin, clichés serve only to call attention to powerless communication.

There may have been a time when a cliché seemed clever, but has since degenerated into a useless conversation filler *(thank you for asking; let's do lunch; at the end of the day; it works for me; it's not rocket science; been there, done that ...).* In response to someone saying "thank you," the waiter responds with "no problem."

If there ever was any meaning of substance, it's been lost. Worse, the recipient will probably see indication of serious brain damage having been suffered by the cliché's deliverer. Clichés are no substitute for putting together a few words that actually make sense.

You know other cliché examples. Drenched from a driving rainstorm you hear "think it'll rain?" In response to a request for information, "we're all over it ..." Even better, "it's being done as we speak."

A cliché's sole function is to make the deliverer appear foolish.

Speech registers—without necessarily being aware, you make use of several speech registers. You have also switched among them with relative ease since your early years: "hi, Mom," to a parent; "gotta split man," to a college friend, and "good afternoon officer," to a policeman.

Communication experts acknowledge five speech-register types: *Static; Formal; Consultative; Casual;* and *Intimate.* Only the Formal and Consultative forms apply to The Game:

> *The Formal register* is one-way in delivery, an audience presentation;
>
> *The Consultative register* is interactive, more formal; always applied to Game participation.

When engaged in a selling transaction keep your consultative register on-point. You aren't your prospect's friend; you do need to engage them. A consultative register may transition to less formal as circumstances allow, but is never overly familiar.

Academic regalia—a speech-register example, academic regalia is associated with a particular role. It may also be adopted at times by the same insufferable types who can describe in pretentiously overbearing detail every nuance of a particular wine.

Words or phrases like *albeit, peruse, fulgent, indeed, incur*, or *so to speak, if you will* ... when used in an academic environment are harmless. But, unless your intent is to convince someone after 5:00 that you are a professor of something or other, leave the *so to speak*s and *albeit*s out of your vocabulary. There are other equally effective ways to motivate people to move to the other side of the bar.

Jargon—jargon also refers to words used only by a specialized group of individuals. The Game has its jargon.

Status within a specialized group requires learning the group's vocabulary. But jargon used outside the group appears as foolish as academic regalia. A sale transaction isn't a *deal*; a down payment isn't a *down stroke*; customers are not *players*.

If having shown the good sense to avoid obscenities in your speech, the opportunity is still available to bury yourself with jargon.

Throwaways—like boundary words and clichés certain terms are throwaways, conversation fillers with no particular use: *basically, to be honest, how are you today? candidly* ... imply the individual speaking has nothing of substance to say, but is about to say it anyway.

Syntax—no discussion is needed regarding whether *I don't get no respect* will leave the person making the statement appear anything less than IQ disadvantaged. It may work for a West Texas CBr, but poor syntax has no place in a sale transaction.

Beyond the Words—Poor Communication Behaviors

Beyond the words the communication door can just as effectively close when you:

Attempt to read others' minds—"You can't get what you want like that." "You don't get it." "I know what you're up to, you're trying to …" "Possibly you aren't equipped to make use of a service this sophisticated."

Bury them with interrogatories—questions are fundamental to selling, but overly aggressive questioning bordering on interrogation holds excellent potential to switch a prospect's enthusiasm meter to *off*.

Assume you get it—"Okay I see what you mean; let me tell you what I would do."

Trivializing their position—"That does seem like a problem, but let me tell you what happened to a friend."

Provide empty support—"Things will work out; don't worry about it." Empty reassurances may have worked for Pollyanna. But when the stress fairy has just blessed the occasion with a visitation, well-meaning statements are near certainly going to be excessively poor form.

Air quotes—an air quote raises doubt, suggesting the words spoken are somehow deficient. The air quote has no place in a selling transaction.

With spoken and written word effects given their proper acknowledgment, nonverbal communication assumes its proper place—center stage.

CHAPTER TWENTY

Nonverbal Communication—The Real Story

Nonverbal language is the universe's clearest communication form: facial expressions; postures; gestures; voice quality; tone of voice; clothing; hairstyle; the distance stood from someone; use of cosmetics; the way a person sits, stands, moves; the location chosen for a discussion; and silences.

Without conscious thought, everyone filters what they hear for intent. Speech intonations, pitch, rhythm, pauses (or lack of pauses) communicate certain qualities: astonishment, excitement, irritation, sarcasm, bitterness, joking, disenchantment, nervousness, anticipation, authority, boredom, excitement, enthusiasm, warmth, hostility, dominance, anxiousness …

Some people appear to sound better than they actually sound because of a confidently communicated appearance. Other people can sound great, but physical appearance diminishes their communication.

Nonverbal Speech Components

Nonverbal speech communication brings words to life through:

Intonation—spoken nonverbal language begins with the *melody* of speech: voice intonation.

Unpleasant voice intonation is a frequent reason for rejection. Hearing some people speak just gets your back up. Others, through more pleasant tones, seem to have a way with babies and difficult people.

Intonation that leaps sharply up and down in pitch, chops off words, punches at certain words and phrases, or clings to a straight monotonous line, is a prime candidate for attention.

Pleasant intonation coupled with positive body language places the communicator at an immediate advantage; others will mirror such a communication.

Voice quality—whether a voice is pleasant or unpleasant is up to listener perception. No objective voice-quality standards exist, but certain negatively perceived voice characteristics in contemporary English are relatively consistent:

An adult high-pitched, nasal voice—among the most negatively viewed. An adult with this voice quality will be image-compromised;

A voice tending toward volume extremes—too loud or too soft; or

A voice too monotonous, or too melodramatic.

Speech patterns are most responsible for voice-quality perception. Not just your voice, the other person's voice quality may affect how you perceive that individual, affecting your conversation's tone.

Phonological stress—phonology places meaning on what is said by a stress peak, indicating the part of a statement to be emphasized.

As example: say *you told me you took care of the problem,* emphasizing one word. Speak it again emphasizing each word in order until each is emphasized individually. Depending on emphasis, each statement is likely spoken under different circumstances.

The same phrase with no stress? No meaning. In conversational sentences no one part is likely to have unusual importance, but the sentence will have one stress peak.

Unconsciously your right brain pays close attention to others' speech patterns. You have heard the response at one time or another when someone was trying to score argumentative points "Well, those were your words, weren't they?" And your response: "yes, but what I meant was ..."

Use of pauses—spontaneous speech without pauses is not possible. Speech experts identify three types of social pauses as providing 40 to 50% of spontaneous communication:

Cognitive—a planned pause, the cognitive pause allows a speaker time to gather thoughts for additional comment. The Game relies on the cognitive pause to anchor a point, or for a salesman to close a sale through the highly-effective *silent close*.

A pause meant to compel a response is one of The Game's most powerful closing techniques.

Social—social pauses regulate conversational turn-taking. An end-of-sentence pause signals the other person's turn to speak.

Filled—a filled pause is an, *ah, um,* or something of the sort, used to maintain the floor while thoughts are gathered.

The first two pauses are intentional; a filled pause is just dull communication.

In a sale transaction a pause needs to be unambiguously clear to have been intentional. If your selling presentations are being interrupted more often than seems reasonable, consider whether unintended signals are being given off.

And, as applies to the spoken word, nonverbal communication has its anomalies.

The Nonverbal Anomaly

Everything associated with an utterance or action communicates. Not all as intended. Nonverbal anomalies, in the same manner as spoken anomalies, will assert themselves.

Assume you have been asked to deliver an interesting speech in costume, appearing as an oversized chicken wearing rainbow shades. You could be Demosthenes' oratorical equal and surfer-chicken's appearance would demolish your communication.

A mistake of that order is not probable; your unconscious mind knows better. A simple correction would be the costume's removal.

But subtler personal anomalies can encroach on communication. "I have no idea what he said; all I could hear was the incessant clearing of his throat." "Did you see how often he blinks?" "Where do you get a haircut like that?"

Everyone has accented speech, but not all accents are universally favored. Some perfectly acceptable language features in New York City may repulse in Atlanta; word choice appealing to an elderly woman may irritate a millennial.

A foreign accent—say, French—can be fashionable, but, "Doesn't his voice have an attractive high-pitched nasal quality?" is not a probable compliment to be heard.

Most anomalies can be eliminated with attention. But some, like senatorial hair, are permanent features. No one could reasonably object to having a magnificently attractive appearance, a spectacularly perfect body, being endowed with stunning eyes ...

But any are just as capable of distracting from an intended communication as bad breath, missing teeth, poor posture, unattractive hair, or such self-created anomalies as tattooing, face metal, or any of the more avant-garde body-piercing variations.

Early in life an individual endowed with unusually attractive appearance may be able to leverage positive appearance for getting what they want. The downside is that looks' advantage may result in going through life without ever having been motivated to learn how to communicate effectively.

When looks are compromised by advancing age, or overindulgence in a few too many Starbuck's macchiatos, that person may well become linguistically compromised. Fortunately, most will not suffer the pain of such a disadvantage.

For physical anomalies, such as stuttering, acknowledge the condition then proceed without further hesitation.

Reading Nonverbal Language—Social Cognition

No message is too subtle for the Adaptive Unconscious to pick up.

With that knowledge you can pay closer attention to your communication, and to others. Nonverbal communication delivers over half the information in any interaction, for the most part conducted below conscious awareness.

Certain behavioral cues are read without conscious thought. You think "who is this nerd?", or "who does this guy think he is?" just by the way they walk toward you when you are about to meet.

You are likely aware that when a person you are speaking with is fidgeting, or glancing at their watch, it's probably best to get to whatever point you set out to make.

Nonverbal communication skill is capable of spotting what in sports and poker vernacular is referred to as a *tell*, an unconscious nonverbal sign that lets you know what may be happening: raising of an eyebrow, change in voice pattern, pauses, shift in posture, questions asked …

Attention to only a few nonverbal characteristics—defensiveness, stonewalling, contempt, critical, closed, friendly, outgoing—tells much of what needs to be known in an interaction, but requires tempering:

Pay attention to the other person's behavior, without reading too much into it;

Don't presume to understand what the prospect is thinking, or feeling. Maybe their leaning back or sitting up is because last night's celebratory event isn't agreeing;

Avoid the temptation to overanalyze. Just be aware when demeanor changes. If discussion is by telephone pay attention to voice changes—intonation, pauses, changes in pattern …

When with someone watch their eyes, frowns, nods, hands, leaning back, leaning forward, recognizing only that a change has occurred.

Books on nonverbal language can be relatively simple: *How to Read a Person Like a Book,* or highly technical: *Kinesics, Proxemics, Paralanguage, Chronemics*—not a page-turner in the group. But some useful information is cloaked within a fogbank of academia.

As with social styles, a few nonverbal communication understandings can play significant roles in The Game's process. Nonverbal language is expressed in units—*emblems* and *clusters*—any of which can be assigned meaning.

Words have to follow in a certain sequence to be understood; nonverbal language has no order requirement. But if nonverbal language isn't in sync with the rest of someone's communication, a condition referred to as *congruence,* there is excellent potential you will reject the whole thing.

Examples of incongruence would be waving a hand while describing hammering a nail into the wall; describing a spiral staircase while pounding on a table; or Steve Martin's loudly expressed, *EXCUUUSE ME!*

But nonverbal language has its simple communications. The other person may stop talking, illustrating implied disinterest, an action capable of prompting need to speak out in defense. But it could also be that they have the information needed, and are considering their decision. The only legitimate of-the-moment response is silence.

Making Others Comfortable with Your Nonverbal Language

Some useful face-to-face nonverbal applications include:

Mirroring

Face-to-face rapport can be engaged through *mirroring*, an action matching your movements in near unison with the other person's moves.

Mirroring can stimulate a sale prospect's opening up to you. Just don't try mirroring in casual conversation; the appearance may be that you're putting the other person on.

Imaging

A tense situation can also be eased by assuming a relaxed manner, a process called *imaging*.

With imaging your speed of movement slows, your tone of voice relaxes—the effect, calming. Imaging is particularly valuable when a sale transaction is by telephone contact, assisted by an on-line web demonstration.

Use of Gestures

Nonverbal communication includes gestures. Referred to by linguists as *emblems*, gestures, like words, have independent meaning—as in the *V* sign for victory, or peace.

Emblems name particular body-language units—position, facial expressions, movements. Linked together emblems form *clusters*, illustrating what is being said.

An emblem can be deliberate or unconscious. But, under either, something is behind the action. Expect at least one of these gestures when an idea is expressed:

Illustrators—deliberate movements acting out what is being said, sometimes with an exact translation into words; among the more universally translatable, *time-out*, illustrated with two hands.

You know others, some kept for special occasions such as unsatisfactory traffic encounters. Describe a spiral staircase to someone without using your body. Try it.

Effect displays—facial expressions—such as a smile, or a frown, illustrating emotions. Effect displays can be deliberate, or unconscious.

Regulators—automatic acts managing interactions. Another person knows they have your attention by your nodding indicating that you're listening.

Adaptors—non-deliberate, connecting what is being said with some action—jabbing at the air with a pencil as you speak of being, really … TICKED!

Researcher Manfred Clynes' extensive body-language studies have concluded that certain forms of emotion, such as rage and hate, contain sharp jabs, dips, and deviations. Actions corresponding to reverence and love are illustrated in smooth unbroken curves.

Mr. Clynes reduced his findings to two simple nonverbal language rules for everyday use:

Avoid angular movements;

Emphasize smoothly curved movements.

Clynes' rules eliminate aggressive actions: shaking the index finger; jabbing at the air with the edge of your hand; or pounding with your fist.

The exception is a movement that is consciously used to illustrate an action. But, even then, minimizing angular body language makes sense.

Other than to a body-language specialist, these terms are not likely to be of significant interest. But selling competence relies on awareness of them.

Developing a Positive Voice Style

While you are paying attention to your prospect's communication their right-brain sensors are assessing: how you are standing or sitting; how your hair is combed; your facial expressions; your eyes, looking directly at them, or to the side; the crease in your slacks; your shoe color ... Shoes shined? Worn? Laces tied?

Physical appearance's importance to initial impression can't be overstated, but voice quality provides an even more telling clue, communicating: nervousness, anticipation, authority, boredom, excitement, enthusiasm ... Your tone of voice: weak? Confident? Warm? Cold? Arrogant? ...

For most people voice quality is treated as just *a part of the way I am* until they hear a recording of themselves. "Do I really sound like that?"

The question to ask is, if you were to spend some time listening to your voice, would you be somebody you would like to listen to? And would respond positively to?

It's reasonable to spend time with your voice. With only minor attention you may find your voice carries more weight. You may also discover that your voice sounds pretty good to you.

A simple exercise uses a recorder while driving, telling the recorder anything—where you're going, about the weather, your thoughts, describe a movie, or something seen in the street—speaking in a normal voice. Later, with quiet time, objectively listen to how you sound. What was said is not relevant; only how it was said.

Is your voice: full, or thin? Confident, or shaky? Personal, or distant? Fast, or slow? Flat, or full of enthusiasm? Again, using your recorder, describe your voice to yourself. Consider how to improve on what you just heard, by:

Picking up the pace if you sound slow;

Slowing the pace if you sound like a pharmaceutical commercial disclaimer;

Eliminating speech-weakening passive words;

Eliminating *uhs, ums, you knows*, and *likes*;

Adding intonation if you sound like you're making a hostage tape;

Getting your voice up if you are speaking in the bottom of your throat, unable to make use of intonation;

Lowering your voice by speaking from your diaphragm if your voice is high-pitched and nasal;

Speaking up if you sound wimp-like;

Easing up on the volume if you sound like a public-address announcer;

Lightening up if you sound uptight;

Toning it down if you sound too flippant.

Repeat the process. Speech characteristics not heard before may be apparent this time. You may find that your voice deepens when you relax. You may also detect a pause before speaking certain words.

Your words will come more easily as you let your thoughts flow. And your speech will reflect the suggested improvements.

CHAPTER TWENTY-ONE

Developing Listening Skill

Active Listening

Identifying need is fundamental to a selling transaction.

Without discovering need, the only option is to just proceed *as if.* You pretend that you already know a prospect's need, or the need isn't relevant to what you have to say. The difference in a sale transaction's outcome is potentially profound:

In the first instance you are tuned in—the prospect's need confirmed, their confidence and trust established; or

You charge into the fray, gun's blazing—the transaction's point obscured by clouds of irrelevance.

One approach requires active listening; the other, just boorish behavior. One takes dead aim at the Duck; the other sticks a gun out the window, and pulls the trigger in the hope a duck flies by at that moment. Lack of thinking is not the problem. Many who are ineffective at The Game are ineffective because they don't know how to stop thinking, and listen.

Listening extends through a series of states:

Detached: not listening. Particularly useful when subjected to a harangue, or a random stream of consciousness directed at you by someone who has little to say, but insists on saying it anyway.

Disinterested: "*Oh, sure I know what you mean. I understand. No need to go on.*" Repetitive stories including *like I said* ... enough times to make the phrase, *I get it!* more pleasurable when delivered in a tone of voice just below a shout.

Selective: selective listening applies to any after-hours watering-hole know-it-all. When someone has little of interest to say, to avoid offending you listen selectively.

Active: attention is full-on; your focus is *there.*

Feedback: listening's highest form. You confirm your understanding. With their position restated, as you understand it, their point is clarified for both of you.

Professional communicators make habitual use of confirming the other person's position through Wordsworth's *wise passiveness,* listening carefully to an incoherent statement. No emotion, just a Zen master's *Beginner's Mind.* The prospect's position is understood—before you speak.

Use of feedback isn't a natural behavior. It's learned:

Without any preconceptions, hear what is said: keeping an open mind, listen to what your prospect is actually communicating;

Restate your understanding of what was said: involvement, pure logic. Feeling is still to come;

Consider your gut feeling: you have heard their words, sensed their meaning, now ...

Finish it: rephrase your understanding. "You apparently have strong feelings. Let me see if I am clear." You're on their wavelength.

Now, with your prospect open to what you have to say, avoid limiting, inconsiderate behavior.

Listening Limitations—the Kind You Place On Yourself

Several common communication behaviors are significantly limiting:

Excessive verbosity: Individuals with little to say attempt to hide their words' lack of substance through word volume.

Assumption that you can anticipate how others will feel: Psychologist David Premack's *Theory of Mind*—an individual's personal view is presumed to also be someone else's thinking. A mind-theory enters into the sale process by a predetermination: "If I do this, they will think that, then they will do ... what?"

Sometimes mind-reading attempts try to interpret facial expressions. Squinting eyes, clenched jaws, a face the color of a Hawaiian sunset may indicate that you are confronting an agitated individual.

When the expression is a smile (a real smile, not a condescending *crocodile smile*), congeniality is assumed. Simple enough. But facial expressions aren't always available.

When you speak on the telephone, write an email or business letter, or think about someone far away, a mind-theory tendency may imagine a prospect's reaction to be what is assumed would be your reaction under the same circumstances.

Assuming you can guess how someone would feel, *if pushed,* places a governor on the ability to close a sale. Mind-theory has no place in The Game.

Lack of understanding relevant terminology: Learn to fluently speak industry language. Cultivated knowledge of your product and its environment speaks well of your credentials.

Imposing your preconceived viewpoint: among the potentially more devastating communication barriers, personal thoughts imposed on someone's meaning is classic. Your biases distort their intended meaning.

Viewpoints are opinions. Whether voicing a viewpoint in agreement, or disagreement, the result of either can be destructive under Game conditions.

Giving in to distractions: The fly buzzing in the corner, the root canal scheduled this afternoon ... even the slightest show of inattention, implies disinterest, and there will be little else to save the day.

Not holding up your end of the conversation: Speaking with someone who doesn't respond to your communication is like shouting up an empty alley. You will feel foolish, and quit. Responses such as "I see," "Tell me more," or a nod of the head, show you are listening.

Inattention to the real message: Experienced communicators place as much attention on what is *not* said as on what *is* said.

The prospect's words are "It all sounds good," but with a slight catch in the voice. The possible real message: "It's out of our budget."

So you follow with "let's consider your options." The prospect gets what they can through the budget; you have a satisfied customer.

Judgment: Some may be offended when they are addressed in a form appearing that they may have said something unintended or are being accused of having taken a position, even if you are absolutely convinced it's exactly what you heard them say. Responding with *you said* may imply an unintended accusative tone, giving the appearance of taking issue.

Playing the Part—a Listener of Uncommon Competence

Average speaking rate is between 110 and 150 words per minute; thinking, four to five times that rate. An apparent consequence is that listener attention, prone to wander, picks up about half the message. But counseling professionals recommend reducing the problem by:

Placing undivided attention on the moment at hand: don't stare. Do smile, nod, encourage ... If a sale call is by telephone, take care the line doesn't go dead on your side when the conversation ball is in the other's court. Give signs that you are listening.

Concentrating attention on the main idea: you have determined how you will approach solving their need; remain on point.

Confirming your understanding of what they had to say: not necessarily in agreement, just that you understand their position. Beginning with *as I understand,* or *my understanding of what was said is* ... will allow the other party to say *yes, that is what I said,* or *no, what I meant was* ...

Keeping it clear: selling communication relies on to-the-point clarity. Leave out ambiguity.

Staying with the standard; avoiding the offbeat: everyday language ranges between formal and informal; regular, and offbeat; general, and specific; orthodox, and heretical, each applied under particular circumstances.

But some are more prone to be drawn into those oh-so-current terms: *dude, geek, psyched, funky, I'm down with that* ... These of-the-moment terms grow stale quickly, but don't disappear soon enough for most to make judgments about the user's maturity.

"But," you may ask, "What if the natural me is more with it than conformist?" Then go ahead. Be whatever your preference calls for. But understand, a heavily opinionated selling style is no cinch to develop.

What may seem as expressing your individuality may actually be an egocentric disinclination to accept The Game's discipline. *Avoiding a patronizing style:* competent selling is not solicitous. An overly solicitous approach has the appearance of questioning a prospect's intelligence. Be respectful, but end it there. You don't need to become their friend.

Making your concern pure: sympathize with the prospect's need; go straight to how you will solve it.

Avoiding use of empty words and meaningless phrases: at the end of the day, candidly, truthfully, hopefully, in the final analysis, they say, the fact is ... were worn out long before they came into common use.

CHAPTER TWENTY-TWO

Dealing with Difficult People

The Game can occasionally require meeting and dealing with really strange, probably not truly dangerous, but sometimes scary individuals.

When you encounter these people, deal with them as though you own them. Back down? No. Definitely not an option.

Most people are reasonable in their communication provided the unwritten rule, *Deal with me as I want to be dealt with*, isn't violated. But there are exceptions: people who play by different rules. These difficult-to-deal-with people will, on occasion, pose a challenge beyond the usual:

An openly-hostile, attack-dog style; and

A polar opposite, the passive-aggressive, capable of disguising their thoughts through profound insincerity.

Openly Hostile Individuals

Dealing with hostile behavior is less difficult if the hostility is accepted as probably not personal. Short of your having resorted to some really poor behavior prompting a reaction, hostility encountered will likely be for other reasons. Two of the more important are:

Free-floating hostility: A component of *Type A* behavior, free-floating hostility is real, used by chronically aggressive personalities to gain the upper hand in a transaction. It's not personal, but can appear personal.

Cold call selling will occasionally encounter congenitally disagreeable characters who resort to an abrasive style as a defense against any sort of intrusion. Individuals possessed of chronic free-floating hostility are easily disturbed, angry, and irritated over just about everything, most of the time.

Stress-response reactions: A stress response can be encountered as a result of your misfortune of being the next caller after the person being contacted has, just prior to your contact, had a furniture-breaking argument with someone; been given bad news; or is just at the end of their tether as a result of a day filled with event overload. *I'm having a day of it, the dog isn't available to kick; you will do.*

With a stress response you are the unlucky recipient of what has been building inside the person contacted, who is now in need of a vent. Unlike free-floating hostility, a chronic behavior, control is not the issue with a stress response.

Both are sudden, but need not be overwhelming so long as the mistake of responding in kind is not made. You may be churning inside, but good sense requires that you neither back down or rise to the bait. Maintaining an outwardly calm demeanor communicating appearance of complete control, you remove yourself from the encounter to return another day when heads are cooler.

When hostility strikes those moments are made easier with realities recognized:

Emotional flooding is probable: in his moment of meltdown, Mr. out-of-control's version of reality may be held onto with furious intensity; no time to reason with Godzilla.

Emotionally flooded people are incapable of acknowledging any version of conditions other than their own, no matter how differently they might see things under other circumstances.

Any statement of appeasement—"you're okay," "everything will be fine"—will be taken by the outraged individual as a personal challenge, requiring that a price be extracted for the indiscretion.

No matter how distorted the position, there is logic: the agitated individual's reality has sense. Resisting the temptation to fight back, acknowledge the other's position, "I hadn't thought about it that way." Then vacate the field.

Chances for returning another day under more favorable circumstances will be considerably improved.

You can't fix it: the ego likes to step in:

"Listen to me ... I know how you feel ..."

"You're not seeing things clearly ..."

"Hear what I'm saying ..."

"I know what you're thinking ..."

An "I can fix this" temptation opens a likely unintended door; the stress carrier assumes you have taken responsibility for correcting the perceived outrage. Demands proceed to the only logical next step: they get worse.

Sympathizing will trap you: keeping statements simple, get out of the situation: "I've caught you at a bad time. I'll check with you next week." Use neutral speech. Leave any mind-theory reference (to how you assume they likely feel about things) out of it.

With all, the objective is to avoid worsening circumstances.

Dealing with the Passive-Aggressive

The passive-aggressive is the master of silence. Most particularly when he disagrees.

No pleasure is to be gained from interaction with Vesuvius-in-the-flesh. But, appearances aside, the passive-aggressive can be the more difficult of the two to deal with. The irrational, emotionally flooded individual can be just about anyone, sometimes. But the façade can eventually be penetrated. Not so the passive-aggressive.

A passive-aggressive behavior staple is profound insincerity; the aim is to avoid disclosure. For the moment, to say whatever seems to appeal even if no intent is attached to following through with a promised action. That aspect of a passive-aggressive individual's behavior makes them a moving target.

Call a passive-aggressive on a commitment not kept, and they will provide perfectly reasonable sincere support for the transgression. Backed into a corner there will be denial of agreement in the first place, or they may burst into a rage for having been outed.

Pathological Liars

At the passive-aggressive universe extreme is the pathological liar, an individual who comes closest to possessing the ability to convince anyone of their sincerity.

Notably proficient at truth distortion, pathological liars are superb communicators. Con men and con women are eloquent, fully capable of giving the impression of complete congruence between their words and nonverbal language.

The more easily a component of communication can be voluntarily controlled, the more effectively it can twist the truth. To spot a lie, watch for a communication mismatch between the words spoken, and, the more difficult to control, voice.

The words of a lie can be worked in advance until perfected ("Now listen to me. I did not ..."). But the face is less easily voluntarily controlled; brief, uncontrolled facial expressions are giveaways, voice intonation control even more difficult.

The ear is better at hearing lies than the eye is at seeing them. Voice pitch tends to rise, and intonation gives away the pathological liar's favorite form of disarming style—highly elliptical speech. For detection of lies pay attention, in descending order, to the speaker's voice, face, body, and (least of all) words.

Fortunately, truth distortion is detectable. Lying to someone suspecting nothing is not the same as when someone is aware. No amount of sweet talk will disguise abnormally heavy stresses on words, or parts of words. A sneer, a smirk, a snarl in the voice appearing nowhere in the words used, and not immediately apparent in facial expressions, is heard.

CHAPTER TWENTY-THREE
Eliminating Communication Barriers

Most communication barriers are removed by entering into a transaction on the right foot. A few options are capable of easing communication issues:

Eliminating the Communication Bypass

A communication bypass results when two very different understandings of a subject are claimed by each party to have been the agreed viewpoint. One of the most prominent manifestations is immediately recognizable: "I know what you think I said, but what I meant was ..."

Communication bypass typically involves what the other person is to get, when they are to get it, at what price they will get it, and under what terms they will get it. The familiar phrase, *the difference between a buyer and a seller*, had its probable beginnings here.

Bypasses usually result from picking out a conversational detail best supporting a position, then staking a claim to the point. A common bypass results from *mitigated speech*, an attempt to sugarcoat a potentially contentious statement. There is no more tenuous form of communication than mitigated speech when absolute clarity is essential.

Avoid bypassing by making a clear statement of your position, then feeding back your understanding of a prospect's *real* position before acting.

Avoiding Communication Blocks

Communication blocks occur when a line is drawn: "I'm not going to discuss it any further." "That's my position; take it or leave it." "You don't know what you're talking about ..."

Standing on principle, communication blocks are poison to a sale transaction.

Avoid creating blocks by knowing when to back off from pressing an issue; when to delay a decision until a cooler head emerges.

The Rule of Agreement

A Game staple: *find common ground with a prospect's position.*

There is no need to take issue with negative response to a premise when the response is turned into supporting the position challenged:

Objection: "We don't need your service."

Response: "That seems apparent; you've done well without us. But our support is an advantage any competitor with ambitions to develop a business like yours would like to have."

Objection: "We're satisfied with the service we have now."

Response: "My reason for calling was an assumption—your business relies on access to good information. We support companies like yours, companies already making good use of the type of service you are currently using.

But you *need* to see what we have. Five minutes! If after five minutes you aren't impressed, the discussion will end. When is the best time for you?"

Objection: "Your competitor's pricing is more reasonable."

Response: "If lower price is your objective, you're better off with their product. But if bottom-line improvement is the objective, that prize belongs to us."

Behavioral Versatility

In the process of developing your personal brand you will develop your own "voice." Just be careful that the voice is not so original that prospects will be put off by it.

It can be assumed that almost anyone will be placed on their guard when a salesman comes on as though they are old friends. No social style will permit getting close that fast; three quarters of the population will react with finality—"This transaction is over."

Adapting your behavior to your prospect's social style is common-sense. Just keep things neutral until their social style is determined.

Beyond developing a personal brand capable of approaching The Game with extreme competence, you can't talk about winning at The Game without mentioning face time with prospects.

Efficiently organizing time to be applied to the process will be to your extreme advantage.

PART SIX

MAKING TIME WORK FOR YOU

CHAPTER TWENTY-FOUR

Time Management's Role in The Game

About Time Management

Recognizing personal brand development's importance, no other part of Game strategy is more relevant to succeeding in the sales role than how time is dedicated to the activity; productive time use is an accomplishment prime-determinant.

Time will be spent on what you unconsciously accept, or consciously choose. Work ethic, and how time is spent, go hand-in-hand, addressing:

Goal setting: volumes have been written on goal-setting's importance to achievement. When goals are not set, *whatever happens, happens* is a well-used cliché;

Daily organization: immediate tasks to be addressed, and their priorities. Getting work done efficiently is a necessity to big production;

Activities monitoring: assessment of how time was spent.

Time management's usefulness is in balancing time between business, and personal, activities.

If immediate gratification has been habitual, time planning can be life-changing. Adopting a more long-term view that sees career development as a series of progressions, will evolve as a revised normal routine.

How You Will Get the Most Out of the Time Available to You

Time is a commodity, an indiscriminate equalizer, a formidable arbiter … also, it's *your* time.

Control over this aspect of personal effectiveness begins with an assessment of how time is to be applied to productive activity, and how the daily 24 hour balance is to be allocated.

Like any commodity, time:

Has value: time's value applies whether productive—business, personal development, exercise, recreation—or absorbed by mindless activities; and, as such,

Is a currency: the term *spending time* is universal. Time is invested in chosen activities, or lost to an array of random options;

Is used as you choose, or are willing to accept: time-use is personal. There isn't enough time to do everything, but plenty of time is available to do the most important things.

Productive time is protected by directing time used to the 20% of activities holding potential to result in 80% of outcomes you expect to achieve.

Game success results from acquiring skills supporting the roles a salesman routinely plays: administrator, public relations specialist, planner, counselor, and barnyard psychologist. All require clock-time spent supporting the salesman's primary function—a driving force behind sales production.

In the best of conditions, the absolute ideal is to define boundaries around your activities: when you are at work, keep your head in the work; when you're at home, or at play, keep your head there, and only there.

Sometimes circumstances require calling a customer from the gym, or checking with a family member between meetings. But the more you blend your life, the more mixed-up, distracted and overwhelmed you will likely feel and act. With fewer interruptions you will feel more balanced.

In the extreme, time management gurus often suggest strategies for getting the most out of every day's every minute, a concept similar in practicality to a rigid diet of root vegetables and spring water, without room for the occasional indulgence in the Colonel's Extra Crispy.

But, giving time management its proper attention, optimizing use of the week's 168 hours is common sense.

Authors on time management subjects, while not in complete accord on everything, generally agree on a few strategic priorities:

Get organized: top salespeople are better at managing themselves, and making needed adjustments to the selling environment. Define what needs to be done, then monitor what was intended, in context with actual results.

Protect how your time is spent: time allocated for business activities is *prime time.* But every day may also include time dedicated to social, family, and personal preferences. With planning, no activity need encroach on the others.

Goal focus: time-management strategists stress the importance of written goals, supported by monitoring progress. High-performance types set worthwhile objectives: long-term, where you would like your career to be in five, 10, 20 ... years; achievable intermediate step goals; and daily goals, defined by a task list.

Eliminate poor time-related habits: unproductive time usage is easily corrected with a simple time-management system. But excessive inability to manage time may result from procrastination—a habit of putting things off until they erupt into crisis.

Procrastination is a behavior, capable of being brought under control through habit modification, unless the problem results from ADD/ADHD, possibly requiring professional help to overcome.

Under either condition, procrastination's symptoms are destructive, resulting in: difficulty organizing; trouble starting a project; having several projects in process simultaneously; or a struggle with follow-through. Any will result in a notably undesirable outcome: underachievement.

Spending Time Well

The great free gift is time keeps coming, day after day. It will be used as consciously directed, or consumed by random attention-grabbers.

While pursuit of your Game activities can, and should be, pleasurable, the term *mixing business with pleasure* is an oxymoron.

Business pursuits have a point to them; pleasure in this sense implies relaxation, away from routine. No one wins when you routinely run your family's carpool from your office phone, or email customers from the soccer field.

Consciously planned, or randomly applied, there can only be so many ways to slice up a day:

Family/social: Time spent with family or friends, recharging the emotional batteries, is essential to life balance.

Recreation: Recreational activity takes in time spent on non-work-related subjects that make you a more interesting (and interested) person: museums, concerts, art exhibits, regular physical exercise ... Any also least likely to happen without making time specific to the event available.

Business/Professional: Professional activities encompass personal brand development, business development, and administrative support.

Prime time usage most capable of directly affecting Game-related activities includes:

Personal Sales Production:

Identifying high-potential prospects;

Prospecting/cold calls;

Key prospect follow-up contact;

Presentation development/associated correspondence; and

Sale negotiations.

Administrative Activity—directly affects production support:

Transaction management, following through to a sale's conclusion;

Market research;

Customer relationship management; and

Existing client support.

Education—early personal effectiveness growth correlates directly with clock-time spent on professional education:

Industry information available through print publications and the Internet;

Industry event attendance relating to your business activity; and

How-to books on subjects of importance to your Game competence.

Similar to physical fitness, education holds a high probability of landing in the likely-most-neglected category of how time is spent.

Networking—regular contact with active industry participants—budgeted in the same manner as any other Game activity—is essential to developing a touch peculiar to individuals who have attained dominant status.

Free up time to do things you want to do by reducing prime time encroachment.

Protect Prime Time

Procrastination is a highly destructive, and habitual, prime time offender—"giving in to feeling good."

Putting off work activity to play video games or water the plants might seem like nothing more serious than poor time-management. But psychologists maintain that chronic procrastination is an emotional strategy for dealing with stress, and can lead to significant issues in relationships, jobs, finances, even health.

Procrastination—*putting off either starting or completing something previously consciously agreed to*—needs no elaboration. Researchers define procrastination as "The intentional delay of an action despite foreseeable negative future consequences." It's opting for short-term pleasure at the cost of long-term accomplishment.

Delaying the start of a project until a later time due to scheduling restraints, or the presentation wasn't finished over the weekend because of houseguests, are circumstantial. Those decisions apply common sense—not the result of procrastination.

Real procrastination is entirely different, resulting in projects requiring attention to detail not being done well; worse, others' loss of confidence in your dependability. Several reasons apply to chronic procrastination:

Dislike for the task at hand: need to address an undesirable task can result in anxious, even overwhelmed, feelings. The resulting action gives in to a *feel-good* delay, leaving the task for *later.*

Fear of failure: "Why should I spend time on that prospect? They're just going to say no anyway."

Fear of success: strange. Also true. A weak ego—*I'm not worthy*—asserting itself.

Fear of being "found out": competence required to perform the task is not as well-developed as anticipated. You won't measure up to expectations.

Inability to concentrate: too much diversion of attention to extraneous attention-getters: any of the social media favorites, email, or inconsiderate people who have time to waste, and want to waste it with you.

Mental-health effects of procrastination are well-documented: habitual procrastinators have higher rates of depression and anxiety, and a poorer sense of well-being. Procrastination-related time wasters are easily recognized:

I'll feel more like it tomorrow

Putting off an important project until "I feel more like doing it" is a crisis in process. Acknowledge the reality: negative emotions taking over. Then get started.

The act of beginning leads to another step: the desire to address the feel-good attraction of putting off getting started *until another day* is overcome.

Too many projects in process

Jumping from one project to another is a prime productivity

killer. You can't always be initiating, or tasks already begun won't be completed or will be unnecessarily delayed.

Overly-lengthy telephone calls

Limit prime time telephone-call duration. Effective business-related telephone calls are brief, to the point, and ended. By eliminating this particular time thief, you don't just increase your productivity; your stock with the individual you called will rise.

Too much attention to diversions

Certain diversions tend to be viewed as entitlements—email, or any form of web-based social contact vehicle. Any can be useful, but also are excessively intrusive prime-time syphons capable of interrupting what you are doing without regard to the activity's importance.

You can even participate in your productivity reduction by convincing yourself that answering every email, as received, is really necessary.

Overscheduling

Leave room for response to unexpected requirements. An apparently under-control sale suddenly erupts into a crisis, requiring damage control. Whatever was in process, set aside ...

Inability to focus

Creative response to a problem requires uninterrupted thought. Identify an appropriate location and time needed for work requiring focused attention. A project delayed by inadequate time allocated to the task will require additional start-up time when you return to it.

Inadequate work quality

Allocate time sufficient to complete a project right. A hurried approach to work requiring quality of conclusions risks a high probability of having to do be redone.

The philosophical concept, *close-enough*, applied to work requiring an element of quality can be a crushing time-waster when close-enough turns out to be neither close, nor enough. The resulting sloppy effort near certainly will result in a reputation for marginal work quality.

Focusing on time management alone will help procrastinators, but only so much. The problem has to be directly addressed.

Optimize Peak-Time

To be human is to be subject to Circadian Rhythms—24-hour variations in body temperature, hormone production, and cognitive awareness.

Everything in the body gears itself to highest performance at a certain time of day, a *peak-time* daily cycle of mental/emotional effectiveness, with certain periods best suited for particular activities:

Morning—with efficiency peaking for most early in the day, customer prospects are more likely to be most approachable in mornings; customer contact, most productive.

Mid-day—mid-day focus best shifts to selling support—setting appointments, making follow-up contacts.

Late Afternoon—toward day's end activities best shift to researching new prospects, and administrative needs that require attention, but are less demanding on creative thought.

Evenings—when conditions are more relaxed, the end of prime time is better suited for education (reading materials), time planning, and email responses.

Peak-time, when emotional energy is at its highest, is best reserved for projects requiring creative thought: developing productive responses to objections; or conceptualizing an approach to a selected customer prospect.

In defining a plan for peak-time usage:

Consider your personal time's value

With no implication of a *me-first* attitude, simply recognize that it's your time; you determine how it's best spent. The less others are capable of affecting your schedule, the more likely time spent will be organized in your favor.

Leave some room in your schedule

Circumstances change; you can find yourself having committed to a once-future, now-current, event that hindsight would have dictated not doing.

Plan your contact schedule ahead

The Game is a people-contact enterprise. Assess each contact's potential, then prioritize contacts into *high*, *moderate*, and *marginal*.

Priorities consider high-potential prospects and networking relationships capable of influencing others on your behalf.

CHAPTER TWENTY-FIVE
Organizing Time Priorities

Eisenhower's Matrix

Former President Eisenhower is attributed to have postulated "What is important is seldom urgent, and what is urgent is seldom important," a concept later named *Eisenhower's Matrix.*

Important activities are important because they have substantive value; unimportant activities don't. Urgent activities have a pressing deadline; non-urgent activities don't.

President Eisenhower's concept was featured in Stephen Covey's book "The 7 Habits of Highly Effective People," and was the topic of Roger and Rebecca Merrill's book "Connections: Quadrant II Time Management."

A days-end trip home attaching the feeling "I don't know what I did today" supports good reason to evaluate how your time is being spent. If nonproductive activity is consuming too much productive time, time planning will refocus attention on where it belongs—urgency and importance considered.

Urgent and Important Activities

Urgent activities must be dealt with now: dealing with an irate individual; meeting a deadline; repairing a broken copier when you have a monster proposal to get out and the office staff has left for the day; explaining your innocence to a traffic officer ... all are as important as they are urgent.

Some urgent activities are urgent by their nature; there is no getting away from them. Others are self-created. Society's procrastinators have a more than casual acquaintance with an out-of-control schedule.

A time-management crisis results when, not having gotten around to completing a scheduled something or other, it's right on top of you.

Procrastination, a time mismanagement favorite, is often a prime mover in sending an important activity into a crisis mode. But the condition can just as well result from over-promising—"I'll have a response to you tomorrow morning."

Not Urgent but Important Activities

Important activities that are not necessarily urgent often under-write personal effectiveness, and are frequently paradoxical—likely to be delayed until *there is a more convenient time.*

Family time, personal planning, professional knowledge development, relationship-building, time-planning, physical exercise, reading good literature, attending a concert, meditation, networking ... all are activities capable of enhancing competence, and of being leveraged. Each will apply tomorrow, and every day forward.

Urgent, but Unimportant, Activities

Unimportant activity masquerading as urgent is the domain of flagrant time killers; time is spent on other's demands. Appearance is unsupported importance was warranted; in reality the time bank was just robbed. Personal telephone calls, most meetings, junk mail, social media, and drop-in visitors populate this category of time-wasters.

Neither Urgent nor Important Activities

When activities that are neither urgent nor important dominate the moment, the brain is placed on hold. If television is your religion, a big screen your temple, you are likely acquainted with time spent here.

Activities of this sort possess the qualities of a slice of white bread's contribution to nutrition. Avoidance of seriously useless activities is common sense, but there *is* reason for being there. The stress from addressing the day's urgencies can make escape to mindless activity an attractive option.

That doesn't change the fact that time spent on low-content novels, hip hop music, most television, prolonged unconstructive talk, and social media surfing probably reduces quality of life.

The Daily Plan

Plan tomorrow's schedule tonight. A few minutes at days-end to plan tomorrow's priorities avoids the need to scramble the next morning to organize the day.

A time plan's purpose is serious, not a do-at-all-cost schedule, just keeping priorities focused:

Scheduling future activities; and

Assessing how time spent today was actually spent.

A bonus is a sense of accomplishment realized by time having been well-spent.

The concept of a prioritized daily *things-to-do* list is attributed to Ivy Lee, a late 1800s/early 1900s business consultant. The daily list was acknowledged by Bethlehem Steel's president, Charles M. Schwab as "the most profitable advice" he had received.

No matter how efficient you become you will be aware of more than you can possibly do. Assessing what was done with time, after the fact, holds quantifiable value.

Improve productive time by one hour per workday (assuming vacation days and holidays are not included), and you will add six, five-day weeks of eight-hours-per-day production to a calendar year. That six work-week bonus can be spent on optional productive activities—education, prospecting, improving your sales production, or family time.

As compelling as this may sound, a reasonable question is: how much time can be effectively used? An objective of 100% productive time use isn't sensible. Or feasible. There are occasions when good sense is to spend time letting the personal batteries recharge.

Time-planning is vital to personal effectiveness, just keep it efficient. You can't do everything. But you can do much of what you commit to.

Prime-time activities include:

Lead Generation—letters, emails, and cold calling;

Sale Presentations—executing on needs-satisfaction demonstration appointments;

Transaction Management—follow-up activities required to complete a sale; post-sale management;

Education—classes, seminars, reading … on subjects applied to Game effectiveness; and

Administrative—planning, filing …

Prioritize tomorrow's tasks calling for attention. Which tasks are absolutely necessary to move things ahead?

If you feel you didn't accomplish enough today, possibly the feeling is asking: did you really not have time to make it to the gym? Or make that phone call you could have made, but didn't?

Auditing your time will help that assessment. If a block of prime time was lost today, there is no need for tomorrow to be the same.

Enter, Mr. Lee's activity list.

The Activity List

An activity list functions as a sort of lightweight personal manager, directing attention to:

Sales contact development, telephone calls, letters to be written, research to be conducted, sales calls to be pursued tomorrow; and

Current day's completed activitys' results reviewed, and checked off.

Recognizing the activity list as a useful part of time organization, there is a caveat: for the ultra-organized, the list may evolve into a time-consuming task in itself.

To optimize a daily list's value:

Leave out routine tasks—things you do as a matter of course will take care of themselves;

Allow for disaster—even small disasters;

Assume that some level of detail exists behind certain tasks—describing an administrative task in complete detail is unnecessary;

Move not-yet-completed tasks forward—moving an incomplete task to tomorrow's activity list calls attention to where attention may be needed;

List planned activities in order of importance—the best time to do the most important things may be early in the day. Tackle those things first.

Avoid paperwork, unnecessary telephone calls, social media, and unimportant tasks during peak-time. Peak-time spent on easy, low-value tasks reduces enthusiasm needed for high-return activities—prospecting, sales calls ... It's urgent, but not really important, activities getting in the way of activities capable of affecting today's outcomes.

Decide what's important; spend your time there.

PART SEVEN

PUTTING IT ALL TOGETHER

CHAPTER TWENTY-SIX

Build Your Brand

You have the experience of being you. Now you have to have the experience of being a salesman.

Game beginnings start with a grassroots understanding—what constitutes a superior salesman. The objective—build an imposing, edgy style.

But The Game's tacit nature requires not really getting to know it until you have first experienced a few bumps and bruises. Ultimately it will be the result of a human creation, flawed as all human creations must be.

You are not unusual if a selling role is not an immediately comfortable fit. The condition is near universal to anyone who has ever seriously taken on The Game as their profession.

But, at the outset, understand—you can do this—you can do whatever you set out to do. You work hard, you out-prepare everyone else—you're going to succeed.

Skill required of The Game is not perfected at once, you will grow into it. It's not that any of this is hard, it's just new. Initially the experience gap will be bridged by sweat equity and dedication. The process will result in mistakes being made, some with enthusiastically supported preliminary confidence.

But, however they are made, mistakes are conditional to developing a personal brand—for extending beyond simply getting by. No one was ever swept into an impressive career through mediocrity. Obsession with a desire to do a first-class job is a good start.

Make improvements incrementally. Today you get a little better from having made a mistake or two yesterday; tomorrow, what you learned from today's errors will be available to be applied.

And, with growth in competence, cumulative gains will steadily move the needle through every step needed to achieve GameBreaker status.

Like following an unfamiliar mountain path, the learning process isn't a straight line with a clearly apparent end. Along the path you may find yourself feeling restless. When you do, speed up the pace. If you feel overwhelmed, slow down, or stop and rest.

There is an equilibrium between restlessness and exhaustion. Find it.

Mastering the personal development process' path is a reasonable objective so long as the objective remains continued personal growth rather than an assumed reaching of the mountain's peak.

In taking on what may occasionally look like impossible terrain, take it one piece at a time. The need isn't to be super-aggressive, just to develop the courage attached to super-confident. One day the clouds will lift, replaced by a realization—*I can do this.*

Remaining a lifetime student of the craft is an appealing facet of selling; you will always have the ability to improve on what you do. In the end, two participant types define The Game: those who play to win; and the other kind.

In your arriving at this point, observations have been concerned with what, for the most part, has proven effective, or generally acceptable in Game participation. A basic component in your future, distinguishing you from other Game participants, will be the ability to finish the close ones.

Outstanding intelligence is an advantage, but intelligence is only one small part of the package supporting success in selling. Discipline, hard work, perseverance, and strength of character play considerably larger roles.

As your progress develops, every day a better way, even if only slightly better, is found to improve on what you do. Acquiring a few new habits and behaviors will significantly affect your Game competence as you:

Acquire a definite statement of purpose: what type of business do you want to own? You have a plan. You believe it can be done. And you hold yourself accountable.

Having a clear vision of a direction inspires; work becomes enjoyable, rather than a chore.

Go the extra mile: give more, get more.

Expect, and learn from, defeat: expect to be schooled a bit at first. Those lessons learned will serve you well. The courage to fail big attaches potential for big success. Coping with failure builds strength of character, and, with it, confidence.

Develop a likable style: people prefer to do business with individuals they like—people who are cheerful, and considerate

Develop your creative ability: an ability to see something differently than others have seen it will add considerably to enhancing a competitive advantage.

Focus your attention: take the time necessary to do things right, acquiring a reputation for excellence.

Form the necessary habits: habits, good or bad, are acquired in the same manner—through repetition.

Remedy self-defeating behaviors: and you will be much more effective in everything you do. Examples: procrastination; lack of preparation; poor follow-through; not learning from mistakes; being knowledgeable, but lacking interpersonal skills; trying to be liked by always saying *yes,* even when you want to say *no;* having unrealistic expectations …

As you become the hunter, staying in character will support all this becoming mostly easy, your persuasive qualities developing:

A communication of self-assurance: a manner inspiring a trust and confidence that moves people to want to do business with you.

A clear communication of thoughts: brief; interesting; the ability to separate words spoken from their real meaning—yours, and theirs;

The ability to demonstrate good reason to work with you:

> Your knowledge of your prospect's services, and their probable need;
>
> How your product is the best possible option to satisfy your prospect's pressing need;
>
> Other customer's results—mini-case histories; and
>
> Your industry, and competitive-product, knowledge; understanding of available alternatives to your product.

And in the process:

Place yourself into the background: avoid the assumption that some of your accustomed less-desirable behaviors will be acceptable.

Have your story straight: a presentation's main idea, creatively framed into a narrative of the simplest possible structure.

Take advantage of others' successful styles: game language fluency initially enabled by imitation.

Limit excessive use of adjectives and adverbs.

Develop your own power phrases: think Ben Feldman polishing his power phrases in the evening for use in tomorrow's presentations.

Avoid overstatement: amateurishly embellishing a product or service's qualities.

Avoid use of qualifiers: rather, very, little, pretty, kind of …

Keep communication conventional, compact, informative, unpretentious: the message's manner—straightforward.

Develop a killer presentation: have a point, a main idea; frame it creatively—get straight to it.

Avoid flamboyant speech: exaggeration, the pretentious, the coy …

Dress the part: your image—how you dress for the event—makes a clear statement.

Project an air of confidence: actions communicate your certainty of what you have to offer.

With experience some persuasive skills will develop through trial and error; others will require the same careful attention to developing exceptional competence that a sport requires.

Succeeding in sports, politics, computer programming, selling … all have in common that the brain learns the same way—a cumulative sampling of errors, followed by error corrections.

Some Game behaviors, until you become accustomed to them, may make you uncomfortable. But discomfort results only from self-placed limits.

Stay with your rational thoughts. In the end, satisfying results can be achieved by acquiring basic competence in the right combination of skills.

Making your mark in The Game will rely on being your own disciplinarian. There are plenty of things about selling to get you down if you let them. The key phrase, *if you let them.*

Your responsibility will be to:

Get, and stay, motivated: talk to yourself, get others you know involved, write down a few objectives you expect to achieve. Read about others who have followed the same path you are about to embark on, and who have done well in the process

Take selling seriously: like being a champion in sports, an outstanding salesman isn't working a part-time job. Never stop learning everything you can about what you need to know.

Create an affirmation, a statement of purpose: one that excites you. Getting to some sort of pre-eminence assumes a single-minded intent to get there. Print it. Place it in a conspicuous place—where you can see it.

It might include inspirational words taped to your computer, or a statement of resolution of what you are going to do. Read it aloud to yourself every day. In time, it will become part of you.

Try things possibly uncomfortable to you: just reading Game-Breaker will not make you a better salesman. You have to apply what you have learned, see if you get it, make a few adjustments, then try again.

As you get into the subject, take time to digest what you learned, then apply what you learned about presentation formatting to your own preference. You want the material to be a part of you; to be there when you need it.

Stay loose: your first obligation to the process of learning the craft of selling is to enter into a selling career with enthusiasm; on occasion, with wild abandon. Selling doesn't work when it's attempted in the grip of anxiety.

Don't spend too much time fretting over your first sale presentation. Just go for it. When the brain freezes, selling capabilities default to habitual behaviors.

When the presentation's over, evaluate where the need to tweak a few things was made apparent.

Set a calls-completed quota: selling is a process of numbers. Making a certain number of calls each day is a discipline. Most successful salesmen set a certain goal—a number of calls to be completed per day, or week—then stick with it.

Don't give up: the job is going to feel too demanding at the outset. But, if you're good, which is why you're here in the first place, you will grow into it and will be much better for the experience.

A principal difference between successful and unsuccessful salesmen is in one of the oldest clichés in the selling book—the salesman's legendary persistence.

How far you go from here is, like most things, a matter of plain old role-up-the-sleeves-hard-work, and practice. Accomplished salesmen represent a particular kind of success. Their careers defined by long arcs of intense dedication, with strengths building upon strengths.

What Ben Feldman proved was doing 90% of what is required is a waste; you have nothing to show for the effort that took you to

90%. Doing 110% of what is expected is a smart investment; it can pay off with a big reputation.

Along your path to developing characteristics common to the dominating individuals who become GameBreakers, most important is the will to be unique—which just happens to be a prerequisite to the sort of success achieved by extraordinary individuals in all fields.

Resource Acknowledgments

During my selling career I had the advantage of access to an extensive variety of excellent resources, studies conducted on an array of motivational topics by pioneering individuals. These were supplemented by biographical summaries of individuals who had distinguished themselves in selling, and how they had gone about it.

I am particularly grateful to those individuals who have pioneered new areas of thought in human motivation, and to the clever thinkers who have taken old ideas, made them new, and were willing to share their concepts.

By its nature, selling is often overly wordy. New selling techniques, and ways of viewing personal development, have been set forth in an impossible-to-digest avalanche of selling *how-to* books, tapes, lectures, and seminars. Thoughts presented have occasionally been represented as radical new concepts; others, while not particularly radical, still were highly useful.

While the full array of resources used is far too extensive to list here, a few stood out as having been most useful to my personal career, and are highlighted in this book. Included among these are:

Part One—The Game, and The Game's Players

What Is the Halo Effect? Kendra Cherry. About Psychology.com

Outliers: The Story of Success. Malcolm Gladwell. New York: Little, Brown, and Company, Hachette Book Group, 2011.

The Book of Survival. Everyman's Guide to Staying Alive in the Cities, the Suburbs, and the Wild Lands beyond. Anthony Greenbank. New York: Harper & Row, 1967.

The Death—and Inspiring Life—of an Extraordinary Salesman: Motivation: It's Not Ben Feldman's Fault That Life Insurance Isn't Universal … Rick Hampton. Article for Associated Press, December, 1980.

Steal This Plot: A Writer's Guide to Story Structure and Plagiarism. William Noble. Sanger, California: The Write Thought, Inc., 1985.

The Peter Principle: Why Things Always Go Wrong. Lawrence J. Peter and Raymond Hull. New York: Harper Collins Publisher, 1969.

The Feldman Method: The Words and Working Philosophy of the World's Greatest Insurance Salesman. Andrew H. Thompson and Lee Rasler. Farnsworth Publishing Co., 1980.

Part Two—The Sale Process

Personal Styles & Effective Performance. David W. Merrill and Roger H. Reid. London: CRC Press, 1981

The Selected Works of R.B. Zajonc. R.B. Zajonc. New York: Wiley, 2004

First Impressions: Making Up Your Mind … J. Willis and A. Todorov. Article in "Psychological Science," 2006

Theory of Mind. Internet Encyclopedia of Philosophy

Diffusion of Innovations. Everett Rogers. New York: Simon and Schuster, 2003

Multimedia Learning. Richard E. Meyer. New York: Cambridge University Press, 2001/2009

Writing a Novel: and Getting Published. Nigel Watts. Lincolnwood, Illinois: NTC/Contemporary Publishing Company, 1996

Part Three—Managing Personal Development

No Limits To Learning: Bridging the Human Gap: The Report to the Club of Rome. J. W. Botkin. Fairview Park, New York: Pergamon Press, Inc., 1971.

Aristotle's First Principles. Terrence Irwin. Oxford: Clarendon Press, 1988.

Death of a Salesman. Arthur Miller. New York: Penguin group, 1976.

Pareto's Principle: the 80/20 Rule. Vilfredo Pareto. Italian Economist who discovered that 80% of a distribution's results is concentrated into 20% of any particular universe. 1906

Zen and the Art of Motorcycle Maintenance. Robert Pirsig. New York: William Morrow and Company, Inc., 1974.

The Tacit Dimension. Polanyi Mihaly. New York: Anchor Books, 1967.

A Logic of Expressive Choice. Alexander A. Schuessler. Princeton: Princeton University Press, 2000.

Travels with Charlie. John Steinbeck. New York: Penguin Group, 1962.

Classics in Psychology: 1855-1914: Historical Essays. Robert H. Wozniak. Bristol: Thoemmes Press, 1999.

Part Four—Game Psychology

Personal Styles & Effective Performance. David W. Merrill and Roger H. Reid. London: CRC Press, 1981.

The Five Factor Model: Emergence of a Taxonomic Model for Personality Psychology. Nathan C. Popkins. Paper on the subject). Illinois: Northwestern University.

Validation of the Five-Factor Model of Personality Across Instruments and Observers. Robert R. McRae and Paul T. Costa. Journal of Personality and Social Psychology, Vol 52 (1), Jan. 1987

Dialectical Behavior Therapy Skills Workbook. Wood McKay and Jeffrey Brantley. Oakland, CA: New Harbinger Publications, Inc., 2007.

Fast and Frugal Heuristics: The Adaptive Toolbox. Gerd Gigerenzer and Peter M. Todd. New York: Oxford University Press, 1999.

Strangers To Ourselves: Discovering The Adaptive Unconscious. Timothy G. Wilson. President and Fellows of Harvard University, 2004.

Social Cognition: Making Sense of People. Ziva Kunda. Cambridge, Massachusetts: The MIT Press, 1999.

Learning and Behavior. J.E. Mazur. New York: Pearson Education, Inc., 2002.

The Psychology of Self-Esteem. Nathaniel Branden. New York: Jossey-Bass, Inc., a Wiley Company, 1969.

The Individual Psychology of Alfred Adler. Alfred Adler. New York: Harper and Row Publishers, Inc., 1956.

Part Five—Game Communication

The Relationship Cure: A Five-Step Guide for Building Better Connections with Family, Friends, and Lovers. John Gottman and Joan Declaire. New York: Crown Publishers, 2001.

Smart Moves: Why Learning is Not All in Your Head. Carla Hannaford. Salt Lake City, Utah: Great River Books, 1995.

Telling Lies: Clues to Deceit in the Marketplace, Politics, and Marriage. Paul Eckman. New York: W.W. Norton and Company, 1985.

Can't Get Through Eight Barriers to Communication, K. Hogan and R. Stubbs. Gretna, Louisiana: Pelican Publishing Company, 2003.

The Encyclopedia of Communication Theory. Steven W. Littlejohn and Karen A. Foss. London: Sage Publications, 2003.

The Definitive Book of Body Language. A. Pease and B. Pease. New York: Bantam Books, 2004.

Kinesics and Context. Ray Birdwhistell. Philadelphia: University of Pennsylvania Press, 1970.

The Significance of Pauses in Spontaneous Speech, S. R. Rochester. Article in "Journal of Psycholinguistic Research" (Vol. 2, No.1), 1973.

Speaking Skills for Every Occasion. Peter L. Miller. Glebe NSW: Pascal Press, 2003.

Nonverbal Communication Modes. Article, Internet (http://www.andrews.edu)

Sentics, the Touch of Emotion. Manfred Clynes. New York: Doubleday/Anchor, 1979.

Speech Registers. Halladay, Macintosh and Stevens. Paper presented to the Linguistic Society of America, 1969.

Type A Behavior: Its Diagnosis and Treatment. Meyer Friedman. New York: Plenum Press, 1996.

Part Six—Making Time Work for You

Eisenhower's Decision Matrix; Eisenhower Method; Eisenhower Matrix

Popularized in:

The 7 Habits of Highly Effective People. Stephen R. Covey. Free Press, 1989.

And further elaborated in *Connections: Quadrant II Time Management.* A. Roger Merrill and Rebecca R. Merrill. Institute for Principle-Centered Leadership, 1989.

Index